ABU DHABI'S
VISI⬤N
2030

An Ongoing Journey
of Economic Development

ABU DHABI'S

VISI●N

2030

An Ongoing Journey
of Economic Development

Linda Low
Abu Dhabi Department of Economic Development, UAE

World Scientific

NEW JERSEY · LONDON · SINGAPORE · BEIJING · SHANGHAI · HONG KONG · TAIPEI · CHENNAI

Published by

World Scientific Publishing Co. Pte. Ltd.

5 Toh Tuck Link, Singapore 596224

USA office: 27 Warren Street, Suite 401-402, Hackensack, NJ 07601

UK office: 57 Shelton Street, Covent Garden, London WC2H 9HE

British Library Cataloguing-in-Publication Data
A catalogue record for this book is available from the British Library.

ABU DHABI'S VISION 2030
An Ongoing Journey of Economic Development

ISBN-13 978-981-4383-92-9
ISBN-10 981-4383-92-9

In-house Editor: Samantha Yong

Typeset by Stallion Press
Email: enquiries@stallionpress.com

Printed in Singapore by World Scientific Printers.

For our mother, Cheong Meow Har.

FOREWORD

This foreword is in support of my encouragement to Linda to combine her academic research and policy-making work. We share a passion for the story of Abu Dhabi to be written.

Economic development, in general for all countries, and for the Emirate of Abu Dhabi, in particular, is at the core of its transformation from an oil economy into a knowledge-based economy of the 21st century and beyond.

This book is the culmination of her learning when we first got together working in the Department of Economy, now the Department of Economic Development, serving the Government of the Emirate of Abu Dhabi.

Many more books will be written as Abu Dhabi and the UAE progress forward in this age of connected globalisation, information communication technology and deregulation. The public and private sectors are working together jointly to be innovative and creative in a new era of the economic growth and development. More information and knowledge in print is always welcomed.

Salem M. Al Dhaheri
Chairman
Bin Salem Holding
Abu Dhabi, United Arab Emirates
2012

PREFACE

The Abu Dhabi emirate is poised for an industrial take-off as it transforms its traditional hydrocarbon economy, by first delving into an energy-intensive and capital-intensive industrialisation based on its comparative advantage. This is the investment-driven stage.

With capital accumulated from hydrocarbons, Abu Dhabi short-circuits the conventional factor-investment-innovation-wealth-driven stages to leapfrog from factor-infrastructure-wealth-driven to innovation-driven. Diversifying into renewable energy for an environmentally sustainable growth trajectory, its manufacturing and service industries, rural and urban, are knitted as a dualistic cluster-based strategy grounded on its policy-induced competitive advantage. This is laid out in Abu Dhabi Economic Vision 2030 following its government restructuring.

This book aims to document the economic policies and growth process in Abu Dhabi as the largest emirate and capital city in the United Arab Emirates (UAE). Vision 2030 reveals a brand of development model in tandem with a unique socio-demographic environment of natural beauty and urbanism. The book tries to connect the dots, highlighting missing ones and new ones. Readers are invited to draw their own perspectives, and to evaluate and make their own scenarios using this book as a launching pad for analysis, deliberation and further studies.

The main conclusion from this five-chapter book is that Abu Dhabi has done the founder and father of the UAE, the first President, His Highness Sheikh Zayed bin Sultan Al Nahyan proud. Policies for institutional- and capability-capacity take time. However, once globalised, the small, open and knowledge-based Abu Dhabi economy is boosted by its unique people-process-product formulation as a brand for differentiation.

Human resources development remains its weakest link. From education to post-employment, it needs continuous education and training throughout the various transformation phases into a higher value-added Vision 2030. A drive to higher productivity is imperative to rebalance demography and counter a high reliance on a foreign labour pool by establishing a qualitative manpower policy and a mind-set change for all.

Abu Dhabi's brand of a macro-social-cum-macro-economy model in economic development has three unique factors: leadership, no resource curse and population as destiny. Through its hydrocarbon-based wealth and strong leadership for Vision 2030, it is on its way to achieve a diversified sustainable economy and society of first-world standards.

Linda Low (Dr)
2012

CONTENTS

Foreword   vii

Preface   ix

List of Tables   xv

List of Figures   xvii

Chapter 1   Introduction   1

1.1. Why this Book?   1
1.2. Organising Theme and Structure of Book   2
1.3. Abu Dhabi in the UAE   4
1.4. UNDP Strategic Development Programme Abu Dhabi, 2000–2020   6
1.5. Vision 2030 for a Knowledge-Based Economy   11
1.6. Statistical Techniques and Tools   20

Chapter 2   Transformation from Oil to Industrialisation   23

2.1. Introduction   23
2.2. Hydrocarbon, Oil and Gas   25
2.3. Renewable Energy, Green Technology, and Sustainable Development   31
2.4. Industrialisation as Planned   35
2.5. Industrialisation as Practised   41

2.6. Science, Technology and Innovation 54
2.7. Manpower-Cum-Education Planning 58

Chapter 3   Non-Oil Knowledge-Based Economy Services   63

3.1. Introduction 63
3.2. Finance, Banking, Insurance, and Islamic Finance 66
3.3. Financial Sector Development and Capital Deepening 77
3.4. Tourism, Wholesale and Retail Trade 81
3.5. Transport, Telecommunication, and Logistics 83
3.6. Real estate, Construction Services and Business
Professional Services 85
3.7. Medical, Biotechnology and Biomedical Services 87
3.8. Wealth Accumulation 88
3.9. Other Domestic Capital, Direct Foreign Investment
and Technology Acquisition 89

Chapter 4   Enablers in Labour, Laws and Regulations   95

4.1. Introduction 95
4.2. Human Capital Formation and Human Resources
Development 96
4.3. Labour and Employment Policy 102
4.3.1. Emirati Labour 102
4.3.2. Foreign Labour 105
4.4. Emiratisation, Family Business, Small and Medium-Sized
Enterprises 108
4.5. Enabling Laws and Regulations 117
4.6. Trade Policy and WTO 125

Chapter 5   Abu Dhabi's Economic Development Model   133

5.1. Introduction 133
5.2. Main Findings 134
5.3. Vision 2030 Benchmarking 142

5.4. Scenarios   145
5.5. Abu Dhabi's Economic Development Model   147
5.6. Conclusions and Policy Implications   153

Bibliography   165

Websites   176

Index   179

LIST OF TABLES

Table 1.1.   Abu Dhabi vision and stages of development
in UNDP plan.   7

Table 1.2.   Comparison of development options and
results 2000–2020.   9

Table 1.3.   Vision 2030 development targets.   19

Table 1.4.   Urban Planning Council growth projections
for Abu Dhabi metropolitan area.   20

Table 2.1.   Abu Dhabi nominal GDP by sectoral percentage
share, 2005–2009, in %.   24

Table 2.2.   Government Industrial Corporation/General
Holding Company factories.   36

Table 3.1.   Projected visitors and tourists in Abu Dhabi by
airport arrivals.   82

Table 3.2.   Total direct foreign investment by economic
activity, 2005–2006.   90

Table 4.1.   The social cost of labour in the UAE.   106

Table 4.2.   Breakdown of subsidies per annum.   107

Table 5.1.   Sectors under vision 2030 and development
of economic development.   143

LIST OF FIGURES

Figure 1.1   Transforming Abu Dhabi into a sustainable
              new economy by reversing Porter's liner
              3-stage into a 4-stage development model.   14

Figure 1.2   SWOT and competitive advantage.   14

Figure 2.1   Institutional set-up for HCSEZ.   38

Figure 2.2   Whole industrial financing process.   38

Figure 2.3   The programmes and schemes.   39

Figure 2.4   Example of a cluster matrix.   39

Figure 3.1   UAE stock exchanges.   75

Chapter 1

INTRODUCTION

1.1. Why this Book?

From an eighteenth-century sheikdom, since the mid-1960s, Abu Dhabi is already a striking example of rapid change surpassing Kuwait's exemplary growth rate by three times. It is widely regarded as a "rags to riches" case (El Mallakh, 1970, p. 135 and *ibid.*, 1981). One book, entitled From Rags to Riches (Al-Fahim, 1998) explores the city's growth.[1] It was claimed then that Abu Dhabi boasts the world's highest per capita income with Kuwait and the US at second and third place, respectively. Abu Dhabi more or less share the top spot with Qatar now.

There is no guarantee either of everlasting economic growth as quantitatively measured by gross domestic product (GDP) or qualitatively as economic development in terms of standards of living. Beset with piracy and tribal warfare, Great Britain in the mid-1800s finessed a maritime truce among the Trucial States now, the UAE. The rest is history. Piracy only remained in failed states, especially Somalia, affecting the world.

Fast-forward decades later, Zayed Vision[2] is crafted in 2007 into the Abu Dhabi Policy Agenda 2007–2008 (Executive Council, 2007) and

---

[1]Some literature on Abu Dhabi include Abed and Hellyer (eds.), 2001, Al Faris (ed.), 2001, Davidson, 2005 and 2009, Oxford Business Group, since 2006, Atef, 2007 and Mann, 2008.

[2]Without an official enunciation of Zayed Vision, it is surmised as his natural proclivity on nature and the environment, but always human resources development as "people-first"; see *UAE Yearbook 2006* for his quotes and thinking on protecting the environment and education as two of his many core passions, http://www.uae-embassy.org/uae/history/sheikh-zayed.

1

Economic Vision 2030 (Government of Abu Dhabi, 2008). Unlike other cases of economic development, the Abu Dhabi model has already grown superlatively. Beyond megatrends (Naisbitt, 1982), the lingering Arab Spring[3] in 2011, it straddles shifting geoeconomics, geopolitics, globalisation and information communication technology.

To maintain more of the same history of wealth and prosperity, the crux is now between Vision 2030 as planned[4] and implementation. Zayed Vision is given life and substance in Vision 2030 as leadership and oil wealth combined to negate the resource curse.[5] This book explores how the Abu Dhabi story, if started out right, will continue sustainably. The journey is more critical than the destination; reflecting the importance of adapting smartly and continuously to evolving challenges. How well it finishes will be left to be seen and judged by readers.

The literature on economic growth and development is extant with empirical evidence and evidence-based outcomes (Hill, 2002). This book features a narrative style to enable questions and issues to fill some gaps and prompt other scholars, researchers and readers to take a multifaceted approach to portray Abu Dhabi. The narration with anecdotal insights goes beyond consultancy reports, all offering expertise in areas from economic planning to project management.

1.2. Organising Theme and Structure of Book

The book's theme focuses on economic development defined as the mobilisation of land (including natural resources, location and

---

[3]The proximate neighbourhood is wrecked with socio-economic unrest, starting with the regime change in Tunisia and Egypt as further empirical evidence of political and economic transformation as a double movement by Polanyi (1957) which has its critique (Birchfield, 1999).

[4]Planning no longer involves central planning in command economies, but strategic planning as a tool to organise and mobilise resources for economic development.

[5]The resource curse suggests that countries with finite, natural resources may fail to develop in other sectors or squander wealth, bringing financial problems to future generations.

climate), labour and capital resources to attain a desired sustainable rate of GDP growth as laid out in Vision 2030. Quantitative growth and qualitative development (Rani *et al.*, 2000; Schumpeter *et al.*, 2003; Myint *et al.*, 2009) are necessary and sufficient conditions — or two sides of the same coin.

Abu Dhabi attained rapid economic growth through oil with economic development to be more framed around a sustainable non-oil industrial structure. Vision 2030 centers on a creative innovative knowledge-based economy and society. Socio-cultural changes affect the economic development. Simplistically, GDP growth may be the means to an end as economic development in the first instance, blossoming to social and political development, however defined, suited to Abu Dhabi.

Oil is finite *vis-à-vis* renewable energy as alternatives. The fact that Abu Dhabi is extending sustainably as an energy capital from traditional oil to solar, wind and nuclear renewable energy is not surprising, but prescient. In envisioning its next growth curve, tackling human resources development as its weakest link is more qualitative than quantitative. Upgrading capital and labour efficiencies encompasses building the right overall environment in institutional-capacity and capability premised on equity.

This chapter will examine the *raison d'etre* for a different but positive growth trajectory to 2030 based on the economic development framework. Chapter 2 traces Abu Dhabi's growth from an oil resource-based economy to industrialisation. Chapter 3 follows with knowledge-based services including financial development. Chapter 4 rounds up the remaining enablers in labour, laws and regulation. Chapter 5 reviews, compares and contrasts the Abu Dhabi model with others to share experiences and lessons.

A political economy approach is inevitable with state dominance.[6] Both specific interventions and other tools of *laissez-faire* market capitalism are discerned in a more competitive globalised world. This book explores Abu Dhabi within the UAE to fit into the new multipolar global operating system.

---

[6]A group of Arab scholars in 2002 did a report under the United Nations on the Arab world's twin deficits of freedom and knowledge followed by a book on Islamic law and economic development; Kuran, 2010.

Since the global financial crisis (Lim *et al.*, 2010; Steil *et al.*, 2009; Reinhart *et al.*, 2009) in 2008, the fragile recovery in the Organisation for Economic Development (OECD) is juxtaposed with rising emerging economies, Brazil, Russia, India, China and South Africa (BRICS).[7]

1.3. Abu Dhabi in the UAE

Foreign investors and multinational corporations analyse Abu Dhabi in the UAE at a country-level. A brief overview is needed to understand Abu Dhabi's resources, wealth and influence in the UAE context.[8] Abu Dhabi, as the capital city, is the largest of seven emirates in the UAE, comprising Dubai, Sharjah, Ras al Khaimah, Ajman, Umm al Quwain and Fujairah.

As the British prepared in 1968 to withdraw East of Suez by 1971, Sheikh Zayed bin Sultan Al Nahyan led the Trucial States to form the UAE union.[9] The confused prologue had Qatar and Bahrain in earlier negotiations. They opted out, but shaped many compromises in the provisional constitution, parts of which may have been settled differently otherwise, representing an expression of the political *status quo* then.

---

[7] Goldman's Sach's 2001original BRIC has attracted additions, such as Indonesia and South Africa (BRIICS), as more emerging economies come on board, followed by more frontier economies. The UAE is awaiting an upgrade since 2009 from frontier to emerging by Morgan Stanley Capital International (MCIS) to attract more private equity, meeting most criteria except its 51:49 ownership rule for listed firms.

[8] Abu Dhabi has 87% of UAE land area, majority of population (over 30%) and national income (two-thirds, with 94% of UAE oil reserves and 93% natural gas reserves as over 8% and 3%, respectively, of global reserves). Its per capita GDP in 2009 is over $90,000 for 1.6 million population in mid-2009, of whom 25% are Emirati nationals (Abu Dhabi, Statistics Centre, 2010, pp. 17 and 104). The last Census 2005 has Abu Dhabi's population at 1.3 million, with an annual average growth rate of 2.5% since 2001; nationals account for 27.1% of the total emirate population with a median age of 22 compared to 32 years for expatriates.

[9] Six Trucial States formed the UAE on December 2, 1971. Ras Al Khaimah formally acceded on February 10, 1972.

A small digression without the detailed etymology of tribes and resultant tribal capitalism faced by Sheikh Zayed is pertinent. Tribal groups do exist with modern capitalism, not in a primitive setting. Acknowledgment of the authority of a tribal chief is owed to a common ancestor or territorial affiliation. A social distance is implicit. Yet, all are UAE nationals, united in culture and religion.

UAE federalism is unique in power ceded upward by local governments, not top-down federal and public finance systems as found elsewhere. The constitution manifests unity with virtually all the functions of a unitary state. Federal laws are implemented and enforced by the emirates' own set of state institutions. What is vested to the union and what is preserved by emirate-sovereignty may duplicate with ambivalence.

The constitution lacks clarity on funds to be provided to cover the federal budget. Article 127 states that all emirates contribute a specified proportion of their annual revenue to cover the UAE annual general budget expenditure, but without an explicit formula. Neither has the constitution any jurisdiction over the collection of, or contribution of, funds.[10] Clearly, Abu Dhabi's munificence is its ability-to-pay.[11]

Each emirate has individual economic development plans, strategies and policies.[12] The Ministry of Economy and other related federal bodies knit together over-arching, cross-cutting or across-the-board matters for a whole-of-UAE. National defence or immigration is clearly federal. Education or health is both federal and local.

---

[10]In practice, only Abu Dhabi (contributed 91.0% and 91.3% in grants in 2000 and 2005, respectively) and Dubai (flat Dh1.2 billion, 2000–2005) have financed the UAE budget; *UAE Yearbook*, various years, and International Monetary Fund, *UAE Country Report* and *UAE Statistical Appendix*, various years.

[11]Fiscal austerity or consolidation prevails elsewhere. Fiscal space (Heller, 2005) is created by reallocating resources as a return of rationing by some difficult decisions for this sustainable availability of budgetary room. Abu Dhabi simply has more budgetary space than most without as much trade-offs.

[12]A policy in a plan implies both thought and actions as a methodology to achieve a target. It prescribes a strategy as action involving tactics in the detail, procedure and order of how to achieve the desired results particular to the strategy.

The UAE Government Strategy 2011–2013 lays the foundations to celebrate UAE Vision 2021[13] as the 50th anniversary since 1971. Seven general principles, seven strategic priorities and seven strategic enablers are the major focus areas for the government in the seven emirates. It is another matter how various ministries coordinate and work with their local counterparts.

1.4. UNDP Strategic Development Programme Abu Dhabi, 2000–2020

A historical preface to economic planning is the Abu Dhabi Strategic Development Programme 2000–2020 by the 1999 United Nations Development Programme UNDP/DESA Project UAE 96/005.[14] It was never executed, except Dubai which executed a similar UNDP project.[15] Unsurprisingly, despite the hiatus, the UNDP plan for Abu Dhabi has the same elements as Vision 2030 or Zayed Vision in the 21st century.

The UNDP identified issues of a narrow production base, falling GDP per capita, slow productivity[16] improvement, population composition and low employment for national graduates. Generous income distribution in health, education and jobs, other wealth distribution in land, buildings, farms, preferential licenses and shares could be revisited. A macro internal–external financial imbalance in the long-run, if oil revenue stagnates or falls thus disrupting public finance, is unsustainable.

---

[13] Enunciated "We want to be among the best countries in the world by 2021" (http://www.vision2021.ae) *inter alia* be united in responsibility, destiny, knowledge and wealth, including a knowledge-based economy (http://uaecabinet.ae/English/UAEStrategy/Pages/UAEGovtStrategy2011-2013.aspx).

[14] It has a three-part main report and detailed sub-reports on individual sectors and 32 projects, including technical reports in supply and use tables (United Nations, 1999).

[15] Dubai's First 2000–2010 Vision was overachieved, followed by the Dubai Strategic Plan 2008–2015.

[16] Productivity is defined as value added per worker or output/labour input. More low-skilled labour in the denominator cannot generate the desired output; high-technology output needs high-skilled input.

Table 1.1. Abu Dhabi vision and stages of development in UNDP plan.

Stages of development	Period	Main features
Starting point	1970s	Oil wealth
I	1975–2000	Oil-based economy, factor-driven
II	2000–2015	Wealth-based with selected investment drive and emphasis on HRD
III	2015–2030 and beyond	Rich economy with selected innovation drive and technology beyond as adaptation/development

Source: 1999 UNDP/DESA Project UAE 96/005.

While the government plays a major role in guiding the private sector, many "missing markets" include a land market and a flexible labour market. Cumbersome business licensing by a multiplicity of authorities is slowly mitigated by inter-governmental agency coordination to promote investment, business or trade. Vision 2030 echoes the UNDP socio-economic concerns of a mindset change in the next generation to propagate innovative growth into the next S-curve.[17]

The main conclusion is that Abu Dhabi needs a long-term vision and development strategy, not more of the same pathway aggravating problems. By stages of development, the UNDP considered the 1975–1995 factor-driven phase to last till 2000 (Table 1.1). With proper planning and private sector support, it could enter a wealth-based economy as investment-driven beginning in 2000–2005 which will remain for another 10–15 years, then entering innovation-driven as an interesting coincidence with Vision 2030.

UNDP Vision 2000–2020 would grow, prosper and diversify Abu Dhabi by broadening its production and income bases. Targets would exceed $35,000 (exceeded in 2005) per capita by 2020 and reduce

---

[17]The S-curve, a mathematic function applied to technology, depicts an initial slow change followed by a rapid change and then ending in a slow change again when the market is saturated and/or newer technology comes along, forming an S-shaped line when depicted graphically.

oil dependence from 43% to 20% of GDP. The proposed scenario and vision using simple limited economic frames and input–output analytical framework has five options:

I Moderate-high growth and economic stability requires government policy and support to develop hydrocarbon, provide a supplementary cushion to the economy to yield 1.5% real increase or 3% nominal growth per annum of oil and gas component of GDP under the standard path.

II Productivity improvement to tackle population, reduce labour intensity with selective policy intervention in coverage and depth for the main sectors in agriculture, manufacturing, construction, trade, hotels and restaurants, government, other services, and higher labour participation rate of nationals.

III Restructuring and upgrading to build on Option II with changes in a sectoral growth strategy on labour and capital requirement. Two broad orientations are the first based on past sectoral growth strategy mainly relying on real estate and housing, trade, hotels and restaurants, agriculture and finance, and the second on heavy emphasis on manufacturing, electricity and water, trade, hotels and restaurants, transport, storage and communication.

IV Wealth creation proposes a conscious effort to acquire assets which would gain significant value in the long-run, targeting $1 billion yearly for investment in assets to gain $30 billion by 2020 and $50 billion by 2030.

V Rationalise public finance to reduce the government deficit mainly through reduction in labour intensity and target population, as well as greater privatisation and improved efficiency of public services.

Options II and III would produce quite satisfactory results in terms of labour requirement, population size and mix, economic diversification, economic stability (Table 1.2). Combining the two is recommended. Some attention to policy Options IV and V could further enhance financial strength as an important guarantee for sustainability for both Abu Dhabi and the UAE as a whole.

Table 1.2. Comparison of development options and results 2000–2020.

Option/Case	Workers '000 2020	Population '000 2020	Citizens (% of pop)	Citizens (% of workforce)	Trade balance (dh billion)
Standard path	2,054	3,154	21	7	46
I Moderate-high growth	2,064	3,167	21	7	86
II Productivity improvement	1,416	2,325	28	10	63
II Sectoral restructuring	1,171	2,007	33	12	71
IV(B) Sectoral restructuring and high labour participation	1,171	1,965	34	14	71

Source: Table 12.1, Table 3.3 (Main document).

The development scenario includes strategic elements, including higher economic growth, productivity improvement, a proper labour/population policy, enhanced labour force participation rates, economic and financial stability, economic dynamism and private sector development. To date, a population policy remains in-waiting.

Targets include a minimum mean GDP 4.5% per annum (assumed real growth) and a maximum population growth of 2.4% per annum for non-citizens for a total of 2 million in population by 2020. Additional employment and business opportunities for nationals involve 116,000 persons for 2000–2020 or an average of 5,800 per annum and wealth creation of $30 billion by 2020 to $50 billion by 2030 through steady investment in tangible assets. The budget deficit for both Abu Dhabi and the UAE would be erased.

Five priority areas include optimal use of basic resources, consolidation of petrochemical and other viable industries, promotion of investment financing and selected services, regional cooperation, and export development. The supporting framework comprises components in basic economic policies, human resources development and labour force participation rate, private sector development and investment promotion, institutional support, and rationalisation of public finance.

Five basic resources are oil and gas, land and groundwater, strategic geographical location, long coastline, and economic surplus. The planning horizon muddles through oil price volatility, energy, especially gas pricing, new energy and technology, the Gulf and Iraq–Iran war, changing scenarios and unwieldy execution.

For the missing land market, the property law is fitting for Abu Dhabi by 2005. Utilisation and special land uses requires zoning. A coordination and policy-making body will monitor water use, manage demand and balance with corrective measures, and augment with desalination and new water technology.

Abu Dhabi's location as a hub rests on its financial wealth base beside physical infrastructure and logistics. Its long coastline, 200 islands, maritime access and marine resources are utilised in ecotourism. It enjoys location (natural resources in energy), location (land, islands and coastline) and location (strategic to Middle East and North Africa, MENA straddling East and South Asia and European Union EU).

Abu Dhabi's economic surplus estimated at $1.3 billion then, invested in land, buildings and large-sized projects on a build-operate-and-transfer or leasing basis is an enabler. The UNDP notes missing elements in economic consolidation and upgrading, lifestyle shopping and world-class leisure industry, transport network, trade infrastructure and services; much has changed since.

The UNDP checklist includes agricultural modernisation, rationalisation of the public sector's role for economic efficiency and performance with measures to raise productivity, human resources development, health, environment monitoring and control, environment impact assessment for all projects, science and technology base, social development, and quality of life. The same checklist remains in Vision 2030.

Specifically, Abu Dhabi is urged to develop petrochemical and other viable industries, to diversify the dualistic GDP structure of a large 80% dominance of the public sector and remaining 20% of the private sector. The major component in output and investment is for petrochemical and chemical. Again, there is consensus in Vision 2030.

Private small and medium-sized enterprises concentrate on food and beverages, clothing and garments, chemical and construction materials and industrial exports, largely for the regional market. The Khalifa Fund to Support and Develop Small and Medium-sized Enterprises abbreviated to Enterprise Development has a full mandate.

Three important areas in industrial development are petrochemical, basic metals and engineering industries, and capital-intensive, knowledge-based industries. Petrochemical, energy-intensive, capital-intensive industries for local and regional markets need scale economies, industrial infrastructure, and access to technology and market. They face intense competition. Regional cooperation is useful, but the Gulf Cooperation Council[18] (GCC) is fully integrated (Low *et al.*, 2010; Rutledge, 2009; Istaitieh, 2008).

The real need is for a private sector thrust to achieve rapid growth in selective production lines to gain competitiveness. For the petrochemical industry, a two-phased programme first concentrates on natural gas as feedstock (fertiliser, polyethylene and ethylene dichloride complexes). The second phase involves a synergy of production lines using natural gas and naptha. Downstream activity is best left for the private sector.

1.5. Vision 2030 for a Knowledge-Based Economy

Before Vision 2030, the Abu Dhabi government restructuring involved the merger of some departments and new entities created to improve government coordination and efficiency. Some 110 laws and 78 decrees were put together by February 2005.[19]

---

[18]The GCC comprises Saudi Arabia, the UAE, Qatar, Kuwait, Bahrain and Oman.
[19]Abu Dhabi Government Restructuring Committee; see Abu Dhabi Government, official websites, http//www.abudhabi.ae, press releases of the Executive Council, various years, for news and statistics.

By end 2008, a strategic plan for government restructuring involves reducing the number of white-collar workers from 65,000 to 18,000, with electronic or e-government in place.

Three contemporary local entities are directly involved in economic development. One is the Executive Affairs Authority tasked to formulate, incubate and implement strategic policy where required, across all government portfolios. It oversees social, technology, economic and political areas, especially matters arising in the most unexpected way which need an urgent response and decision. More detailed analysis and follow-up may be spun-off or in collaboration with other specialised entities.

The second, the Abu Dhabi Council for Economic Development, acts as a policy adviser to the Executive Council or the equivalent Abu Dhabi cabinet. It is tasked to cultivate a dynamic public–private partnership for open communication dialogue between the public sector, local business and Abu Dhabi Chamber of Commerce and Industry in stakeholder networks. It covers energy, infrastructure, banks, insurance, tourism, industry, health care, education, services, transport, and logistics.

The third is a policy-making and regulatory Department of Economic Development.[20] With some ironing out of duplication and clarity of mandate, both the Department of Economic Development and Abu Dhabi Council for Economic Development now have the same chairman (as originally planned in 2006). More inter-agency cooperation seems at work. All departments report to the Executive Council as the ultimate coordinator.

Partial privatisation of parts of Abu Dhabi Inc[21] occurred with initial public offers in food and water companies (Agthia) in 2005 and Arkan Building Materials Company in 2006, all under the

---

[20]The Department of Economic Development since 2009 was previously the Department of Planning and Economy which was from a merger in 2005 of the Department of Planning and the Department of Economy.

[21]Japan Inc was the pioneer, with government planning, finessing and catalysing industrialisation with its family-owned *zaibatsu*, then *keiretsu*, but has stagnated (Adams *et al.*, 2008). Singapore Inc comprises the public sector and government-linked companies created by sovereign wealth funds. Likewise, Abu Dhabi Inc and Dubai Inc have ownership by state, royal families and sovereign wealth funds blurred.

Government Industrial Corporation, reconstituted as General Holding Company. Fixed at 1-dirham, only Emiratis are entitled in initial public offers for wealth distribution. Widening and deepening the Abu Dhabi stock market to mobilise saving and capital seem secondary as the shareholder culture has yet to take root.

Reinventing or reengineering government is more than a fundamental rethinking and radical redesign, not more of the same to bring about dramatic results and improved performance (Hammer and Champy, 1995). It involves a social contract. Corporate governance applies to the government and Abu Dhabi Inc. Government-knows-best and private-sector-knows-more in public–private partnerships is a knowledge-based economy.

Traditionally characterised by fishing, pearl diving, trading, farming and herding, modern Abu Dhabi economy emerged in 1962 when its first oil cargo was exported. Its factor-driven hydrocarbon wealth buoyed by oil prices has GDP, GDP per capita and high standards of living, safety and security so as to arrive at a wealth-driven stage before the investment-driven in infrastructure.

Vision 2030 for transformation follows Porter's (1980 and 2008) sequential three factor-driven, investment-driven and wealth-driven stages and five-forces of substitutes, rivals and new entrants as threats plus bargaining power of suppliers and customers, underpinned by the role of government and chance as a random factor. It is monetising its wealth in infrastructure-driven with an Asian twist of creative innovation (Fan *et al.*, 2009; Chu *et al.*, 2006; Brown, 2006) in a more competitive globalised world.

Adapting Porter's stages for Abu Dhabi, Fig. 1.1 shows a reversal from a wealth-driven stage already attained from a factor-driven stage to investment-driven, then a fourth twist of innovation-driven or knowledge-driven Vision 2030 to lock-in sustainable growth as its unique model. Infrastructural investment must yield innovation by research and development. It needs research to be more than product development; pure technology innovation more than process model innovation.

Figure 1.2 uses Porter's five-forces to recast into Abu Dhabi's strength-weakness-opportunity-threat as self-explanatory, resonating specific-measurable-attainable-realistic-tangible.

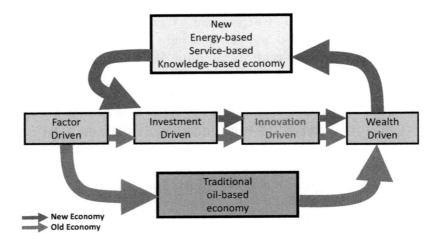

Figure 1.1   Transforming Abu Dhabi into a sustainable new economy by reversing Porter's linear 3-stage into a 4-stage development model.

Source: Jurong International Consulting *et al.*, 2005, Book 1, Diagram 2, p. 27.

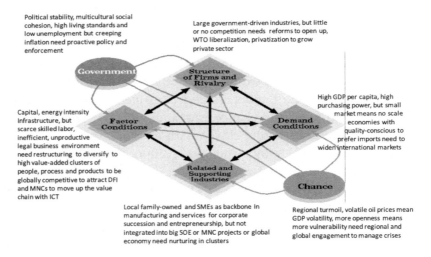

Figure 1.2   SWOT and competitive advantage.

Source: Jurong International Consulting *et al.*, 2005, Book 1, collated from pp. 24–25.

Abu Dhabi's factor-driven comparative advantage is through natural hydrocarbon resources, not labour in a small population where Emiratis are a minority of 20% in their own country. The resultant reliance on unskilled migrant labour may be a cost advantage, but at the risk of national identity, and delay industrial restructuring to more sustainable higher value-added. Mobilisation of labour with changing work culture needs hard policies and quality upgrade for productivity in high-skilled knowledge industries.

A pure resource-based comparative advantage is unsustainable as it is insufficiently dynamic, productive, but vulnerable to volatile world market fluctuations in demand and price. It explains an apparent paradox of Abu Dhabi's drive to achieve non-renewable energy with new energy technology to retain its status as a premier energy capital.

The investment-driven stage had massive investment in infrastructure and industry since Zayed Vision in the 1970s. Abu Dhabi had a five-year plan in 1968–1972, a subsequent three-year plan in 1977–1979 with $612.4 million invested in infrastructure including roads, ports, airports, communication, sewage, electricity and water networks.

The pattern of infrastructural investment reflects the oil boom cycle. Dire basic needs in the 1970s led the GCC, especially Abu Dhabi in the early phases of economic development, to monetise oil gains into infrastructure. By the second oil boom in the 1980s, oil exporting countries' oil revenues exceeded their development requirements, including infrastructure. Having laid the infrastructure backbone, managing facilities competitively is another concern.

The 1980s boom was short-lived, followed by a sharp recession. Crude prices fell to less than $10 per barrel in 1982 which led to government deficits. Belt-tightening prevailed until the mid-1990s, but the cycle is repeated since the 2000s. Vision 2030 seeks to stabilise the gyrations of GDP oil revenue with diversified non-oil GDP, creating new exciting jobs for Emiratis. Neither oil nor middleman-transshipment fits the ambitions of Vision 2030.

Entrepôt trade may suit Dubai as long as its efficient infrastructure and cost advantage are not by-passed by direct trade as other regional ports emerge. Made-in-Abu-Dhabi direct exports from its industrialisation create higher value-added jobs and sustainable skills per Vision 2030. The two economic models effectively complement and supplement to make the UAE globally competitive.

Monetising oil wealth in hard physical infrastructure (investment-driven) is parallel to innovation-driven. Specific innovation policies stress knowledge industries in universities, hospitals, media services and others. Surplus foreign exchange reserves traditionally held in dollar assets are put into new areas, by both geography and industries. It goes further than petrodollar recycling by sovereign wealth funds[22] gearing into commercial strategic, not political acquisitions.[23]

A knowledge-based economy in Vision 2030 is shorthand for using a comparative advantage in natural hydrocarbon resource as the old economy to harness policy-induced artificial competitive advantage related to Porter's five-forces in a micro-environment. An innovation-driven economy is about using intellectual capital as knowledge embodied in skilled labour in an integrated manufacturing-cum-services industrial value chain.[24]

Knowledge industries are capital-intensive, high-technology, embodying superior engineering, artificial intelligence and skills. They can be downstream petroleum or basic steel or integrated aluminium plants and service industries from telecommunication to eco-cultural tourism, construction and utilities in water desalination or nuclear power generation. In adverse terrain and climate, even high-technology biotechnology agriculture has food security reasons given the global food crisis (Evans *et al.*, 2009).

---

[22]The Abu Dhabi Investment Authority 1976 is like the Government of Singapore Investment Company, 1981, managing official reserves, while Mubadala Development Company 2002 is like Temasek Holdings Limited 1974 as a sovereign fund for strategic industrial restructuring. There are international repercussions since the global financial crisis; see Saw *et al.*, 2009, for the definition, origins, growth and impact of sovereign wealth, and also Toledeo, 2009; Abdela *et al.*, 2007; Xu *et al.*, 2010, other research includes London-based The Monitor Group (http://www.monitor.com), Las Vegas-based Institute (http://www.swfinstitute.org), and banks like Morgan Stanley, Stanchart and others.

[23]The Abu Dhabi Investment Authority, the world's largest sovereign wealth fund, co-chaired the International Monetary Fund (IMF) 2008 International Working Group, setting out 24 Santiago general accounting principles and practices for greater transparency.

[24]A typical industrial value chain has research and development, product development, process engineering, manufacturing/production, and marketing and distribution as information like wood as raw material is hewn into knowledge as furniture.

Abu Dhabi's small market achieves efficiency in the business environment through smart technology or production techniques despite limited economies of scale (cost per unit decreases as output increases) or economies of scope (greater variety of products). Greater diversification goes with an export-orientation for markets. It demands global competitiveness, in and of itself as requiring technology and skills transfer to augment Abu Dhabi's capital- and energy-intensity as comparative advantages.

After the 9/11 terrorism, in order to avoid the risks of any Western freeze of overseas investment and in pursuit of financial policies designed to steer assets back to domestically, more multibillion-dollar projects are aimed to diversify national income sources. Domestic capital with direct foreign investment is for technology, management and markets. Petrodollar is recycled East to tap into Asian growth and diversity.

Wealth gained through oil alone is not a necessary condition, but a sufficient condition. The government shifting as a regulator to facilitator in a pro-business friendly environment for overall support and ownership of Vision 2030 is a change agent for the sufficient condition. Doubly blessed with wealth and leadership is a rarity in a virtuous circle versus a vicious circle[25] of poverty and corrupt government elsewhere. But throwing money at the problem is not enough; this creates another set of credibility and image issues.

In summary, three emerging industrial cultures are mutually inclusive as productivity, competitiveness and pro-business environment, all as global proactive and differentiated. Vision 2030 is necessary, yet inadequate without full implementation. Quality human resources development and work attitude must match high-technology industries. Population is destiny, especially for a small, open economy[26] to compete globally.

---

[25]Virtuous circle is a condition in which a favourable circumstance or result gives rise to another which subsequently supports the first, a vicious means one trouble leads to another that aggravates the first.

[26]Expressed as total merchandise trade to GDP, Abu Dhabi's ratio is about 90% in 2009 (computed from Abu Dhabi, Statistics Centre, 2010, p. 17) compared to 200–300% for Singapore and Hong Kong, including services, as the world's most open city-states.

Successful economic development models as benchmarks include Norway as a comparable oil economy, Ireland and New Zealand as small economies. Baseline 2005 sets the targets. Vision 2030 is defined as a sustainable, diversified, high value-added economy, encouraging enterprises and entrepreneurship,[27] globally well-integrated and leading to better opportunities for all. Mitigating some paradoxes, Abu Dhabi's brand of tribal capitalism could join the OECD league with a difference by 2030.

Vision 2030 has two priorities. One is a sustainable economy and the other involves social and regional development balanced across to Al Ain and Al Gharbia (Government of Abu Dhabi, 2008, p. 17). Seven areas of economic policy and 12 focus industries (*ibid.*, 2008, pp. 19 and 113–114) represent an initial wish-list of knowledge-based goods and services.

The 12 sectors in Vision 2030 are energy (other than oil and gas), petrochemicals, metals and mining, aviation, aerospace and defence, pharmaceuticals, biotechnology and life sciences, tourism, healthcare equipment and services, transportation, trade and logistics, education, media, financial services, and telecommunication services. The first seven are globally focused and the last five tap the region.

Five enabling industries are construction and engineering, machinery, electrical equipment, construction materials, and food and beverages. They are defined in various plans and strategy under the Department of Economic Development (Chapter 3) by comparative and competitive analyses, or superceded by faster-moving sovereign wealth funds.

The state picking industries as winners as an industrial policy is justified if market forces as direct foreign investment and multinationals corporations make the ultimate choice. It is not necessarily government protection except for an infant industry justified economically as having potential competitive advantage to graduate by defined timelines. Market forces pick winners; Abu Dhabi Inc facilitates.

---

[27]Entrepreneurship is defined as creative destruction by Schumpeter *et al.*, 2003; and is defined as someone who actually searches for change, responds to it and exploits change as an opportunity by Peter Drucker, 1985.

Table 1.3. Vision 2030 development targets.

Economic development targets	2005–2007	2015	2020	2030
Real GDP growth %	16.4	7.0	6.0	6.0
Nominal GDP growth %	11.8	9.5	7.5	7.5
Total GDP in real 2005 ($ billion)	77.8	167.0	232.1	415.7
Non-oil GDP in real 2005 ($ billion)	41	50	56	64
Non-oil net exports to real GDP %	−23.6	−10.8	−6.6	0.1
Economic concentration % of real 2005 GDP	37	28	24	20
Human capital development				
GDP output per employee $'000	99	114	123	140
National unemployment rate %	12	7	5	5
National active population %	25	34	41	51
National dependency ratio %	3.6	2.2	1.6	1.1
Workforce tertiary education attainment %	16	22	26	31
GDP per capita real 2005 $'000	55.6	65.6	71.5	82.6
Non-oil GDP per capita real 2005 $'000	22.6	32.6	39.9	53.2
Human development index HDI value	0.89	0.90	0.92	0.93
Physical and financial capital				
National asset formation ($ billion)	55.2	113.8	150.8	275.9
Domestic investment to real GDP %	13	18	18	23
Private saving to total aggregate saving %	40	68	74	86

Source: Abu Dhabi Vision 2030, http//: www.abudhabi.ae.

Implicit is a desire for government ownership of hydrocarbon and land as Emirati birth rights.

Tables 1.3 and 1.4 present Vision 2030 targets in statistics, as best as can be gathered. Unlike other developing countries which need statistical data to obtain capital and finance from investors or the World Bank, the UAE as self-financed, and is a laggard in statistics as noted by the International Monetary Fund (IMF) annual Article 4 consultations.

Quintessentially, economic development by diversification is to reverse GDP contribution of oil and non-oil from pre-Vision

Table 1.4. Urban Planning Council growth projections for Abu Dhabi metropolitan area.

	2007 baseline	2013	2020	2030
Residents	930,000	1.3 million	2.0 million	3.1 million
Annual visitors	1.8 million	3.3 million	4.9 million	7.9 million
Residential units	180,000	251,000	411,000	386,000

Source: Urban Planning Council, http//: www.abudhabi.ae.

2005–2006 of 40% and 60% to 60% and 40% respectively by 2030. This needs GDP compound annual growth rates of 7% for 2008–2019 and 6% from 2020–2030. The global financial crisis has slowed GDP to 4.5% by 2011, but as a foretaste, some accomplishments are iconic (Abu Dhabi Department of Economic Development, 2010 and 2011).

Education and health as two pillars in human resources development partner global brands. New York University and Sorbonne University join other Abu Dhabi-based public and private universities. A diabetes centre is supported by London Imperial College. Cleveland Hospital manages Sheikh Khalifa Medical Centre. Saadiyat cultural hub hosts branches of Guggenheim and Louvre museums. With Etihad Airlines, and the world's first Ferrari theme park, Abu Dhabi joined the 2009 Formula One Championship.

1.6. Statistical Techniques and Tools

Abu Dhabi is as wealthy as any first-world OECD country, but is third-world by underdeveloped and undeveloped statistics.[28] Haphazard, confusing, inconsistent and only nominal GDP until recently by many bodies is without a standard methodology of concepts and principles of the UN System of National Accounts, IMF data dissemination system and OECD standards.

It had no statistical system until 2008. The Statistics Division originally in the Department of Planning was spun-off to an

---

[28]For availability of statistical time series, see Abu Dhabi, various years, since 1971 to 2006, and 2010.

autonomous Statistics Centre Abu Dhabi. For the statistical needs of Vision 2030, its five-year plan identifies 629 indicators tracked by over 1,700 reports and over 700 published annually by 2014. Six categories comprise economy, industry and business, population and demography, social, labour force, and agriculture and environment.

Statistics Centre Abu Dhabi aims for updated timely data, consistent historical time series and GDP deflators by updating its statistical frames to 2010 for a population census[29] and household expenditure survey (1996/1997). It has service-level agreements with other data-generating agencies for less duplication, more cooperation and sharing of different econometric models for different specific mandates and needs.

It is restructuring GDP accounts[30] and reported over 50% non-oil GDP share in 2010. It implies that Vision 2030's 2015 target is attained *en route* to its 60% mark by 2030. This GDP restructuring follows the UAE Economic Report 2009 by the Ministry of Economy in 2010, where for the first time, oil GDP fell to 29%, non-oil GDP at 71% in 2009 versus 66.5% in 2008. The UAE statistics may reflect successful diversification in Abu Dhabi and/or Dubai's non-oil performance.

The Abu Dhabi Urban Planning Council (2007) and Department of Transport (2006) need population projections too. Department of Finance's fiscal model forecasts revenue and expenditure. The Department of Economic Development's macroeconomic model has satellite computable general equilibrium models for official GDP forecasts and policy simulations. The General Secretariat is as keen on system dynamics modeling to link up various models for scenario planning.

---

[29]The 2010 census to coincide with others in the GCC was cancelled, but a pilot survey done by June 2011 would restart a full census by September 2011; *Gulf News* 16 March 2010 and 20 April 2011, and *The National,* 13 June 2011. Questions on details of household members, especially females are culturally sensitive with privacy issues. The federal National Bureau for Statistics switched to administrative data from the Ministry of Interior and National Identity Authority to enumerate without the usual census details. The two methodologies are different, respectively measuring stock and flow.

[30]*Gulf News*, May 30, 2010.

Chapter 2

TRANSFORMATION FROM OIL TO INDUSTRIALISATION

2.1. Introduction

Abu Dhabi has three economic sectors (Table 2.1), namely, primary (agriculture, mining, forestry, fishing, hunting, land-related activities); secondary (manufacturing, utilities, and construction); and tertiary or services (including government). This chapter focuses on the transformation of the main traditional primary sector (oil and gas) and industrialisation. Chapter 3 focuses on services and Chapter 4 covers labour, law and regulations.

A dual economy (Boeke, 1953; Lewis, 1954; Oshima, 1963) refers to the co-existence of two separate economic sectors, typically modern and traditional, divided by different levels of progress in productivity, technology, and patterns of demand. The concept exists within the same sector for e.g. in traditional hydrocarbon energy and nuclear power; rural–urban population; and migration *vis-à-vis* modernisation. Inter-industry relationships for multiplier analysis[1] and policies follow.

Industries need raw materials and food from the agricultural sector in a synergistic virtuous circle. The traditional sector is not necessarily backward. Science, technology, research, development and human resources development equally spur rural productivity. In the advanced OECD, the primary sector is part of their high-technology,

---

[1]Input–output tables are more than the supply and use tables (United Nations, 1999) enabling multipliers to show how final demand from one sector spills over to the other sectors to create GDP and jobs.

23

Table 2.1.   Abu Dhabi nominal GDP by sectoral percentage share, 2005–2009, in %.

	2005	2007	2008	2009
Total GDP	100.0	100.0	100.0	100.0
Primary	57.7	57.4	61.7	40.4
Agriculture, livestock, fishing	1.5	1.0	0.8	1.0
Mining, quarrying	56.2	56.4	60.9	49.4
Secondary	16.7	17.4	15.8	20.3
Manufacturing	7.5	6.5	5.8	7.4
Construction	2.3	2.3	2.1	2.8
Utility	6.9	8.6	7.9	10.1
Tertiary	25.7	25.2	22.5	29.3
Wholesale, retail trade	5.2	4.8	4.3	5.5
Hotels, restaurants	0.9	0.9	0.8	1.2
Transport, storage, communication	6.2	6.1	5.5	7.1
Finance, insurance	4.7	5.0	4.5	5.8
Real estate, business	6.7	7.4	6.5	8.4
Other services*	2.0	1.0	1.0	1.2

*Social, personal, government, domestic household, education, and health services.
Source: Computed from Statistics Centre Abu Dhabi. *Statistics Yearbook 2010*, p. 21.

knowledge-based economy. Dualism fits Abu Dhabi except in sectors such as agriculture, animal husbandry, or fishing.

As per the vision of Sheikh Zayed, the traditional sectors should be preserved to promote food security,[2] socio-cultural heritage, and rural development that in turn would conserve the ecology and

---

[2]Abu Dhabi-based, private Al Dahra Agricultural Company follows the UAE policy in food security by acquiring farmlands in Europe, the US, South Asia and North Africa; *The National*, August 14, 2010. Including local farms, with contracts from the UAE government, it controls the entire supply chain with 800 employees worldwide. Al Dahra invests in sophisticated farming equipment not labor-intensive facilitating a farm-to-fork value chain for dairy and farm products, alfalfa and feed grasses. It has spent Dh500 million since 2007 in the US, Spain, Egypt, and Pakistan. Its export markets range from Egypt, Pakistan to the Middle East and Asia. Sovereign wealth funds acquiring farmlands deemed as "land grabs" remains politically sensitive since the food crisis in 2008; *The Economist*, February 24, 2011, special report on feeding the world and May 5, 2011 special report on surge in land deals.

protect the environment. Economic development typically involves workers moving from low-productivity activities like subsistence farming to high-productivity commercial farming. It means weaning off low productivity foreign labour and switching to the knowledge-based economy.

Agriculture continues to occupy a small part in Abu Dhabi's primary sector. Efforts have been taken in generating hydrocarbon (in the primary sector) via the Abu Dhabi National Oil Company (http//www.adnoc.ae and Atef, 2007). On the other hand, Masdar Initiative generates renewable energy. In fact, energy produced by traditional as well as modern means is to ensure Abu Dhabi's emergence as an energy hub which is integral to Vision 2030. Manufacturing share to GDP falling from 7.5% in 2005 to 7.4% in 2009 (Table 2.1) needs to go up to 25% in Vision 2030.

2.2. Hydrocarbon, Oil and Gas[3]

Sheikh Zayed managed Abu Dhabi's oil sovereignty by avoiding nationalisation which was fashionable in the 1970s.[4] The Supreme Petroleum Council[5] oversees hydrocarbon policies and the 100%-owned government holding company Abu Dhabi National Oil Company-FOD that was set up in 1971.

---

[3]Abu Dhabi National Oil Company, *et al.*, 2010, pp. 16 and 59, updated UAE gas reserves to 204.8 trillion cubic feet (slightly less than 227.1 trillion cubic feet published by British Petroleum in its benchmark *Statistical Review of World Energy Yearbook*) and oil reserves as 98.2 billion barrels (higher than British Petroleum's estimate of 97.8 billion barrels).

[4]Abu Dhabi granted its first oil concession, covering its entire territory, in 1939 to the Trucial Coast Development Oil Company (renamed the Abu Dhabi Petroleum Company in 1962). Oil was discovered in 1960; production and export commenced in 1962 offshore and in 1963 onshore.

[5]Abu Dhabi National Oil Company, *et al.*, 2010 has an interview of Supreme Petroleum Council's secretary-general and chief executive officer, pp. 7–8.

Its assets were bought from foreign oil companies in 1974.[6] In this case, International oil companies are not owners, but are operators on a production-sharing basis offering technology and management expertise. The UAE follows quotas and obligations in the Organisation of Petroleum Exporting Countries (OPEC).

Upstream, the main onshore fields are Zakum, Bab, Asab, Bu Hasa, Sahil and Shah. Offshore, the Abu Dhabi Marine Operating Company operates Umm al Shaif and Lower Zakum. The Zakum Development Company operates Upper Zakum and two other fields.[7] The International Petroleum Investment Company and the Abu Dhabi National Energy Company or Taqa pursue exploration and production opportunities outside UAE, including in North Africa, Central Asia, and the North Sea.

A gap exists between oil production and refinery capacity for more downstream activities.[8] Since 1998, the Abu Dhabi National Oil Company has two complementary joint ventures with Austria's Borealis to manufacture polyolefin plastics. The first company under

---

[6]Abu Dhabi National Oil Company acquired 60% of Abu Dhabi Petroleum Company. In 1978, the Abu Dhabi Petroleum Company was reconstituted as the Abu Dhabi Company for Onshore Oil Operations working with Japan Oil Development Company, British Petroleum, Compagnie Française des Pétroles, Royal Dutch Shell Oil, Mobil Oil, Exxon and Participations and Explorations (Partex).

[7]More than half of Abu Dhabi's oil production is generated by the Abu Dhabi Company for Onshore Operations, one of the 10 largest oil companies worldwide and the largest crude oil producer in the Southern Arabian Gulf. The second main producer is Abu Dhabi Marine Operating Company which started in 1953 when Abu Dhabi granted a concession to the D'Arcy Exploration Company of Britain. It was to look for oil in offshore and submerged areas that were not covered in the concession for Abu Dhabi Company for Onshore Operations. Abu Dhabi Marine Areas, a multinational consortium, took over this concession in 1955. The company made its first commercial strike in 1958, with production and export started in 1962. In 1977 Abu Dhabi Marine Operating Company and Abu Dhabi National Oil Company agreed to form the Abu Dhabi Marine Areas Operating Company for offshore work. The output of oil and gas from the offshore company's fields is transported to its centre of operations on Das Island for processing, storage, and export.

[8]For example, the UAE has six refineries in operation which in 2003 exported 0.33 million barrels per day in refined products compared to 2.17 million barrels per day in crude oil.

the joint venture is the Borouge in Ruwais[9] and the second company is the Borouge Pte Ltd which is based in Singapore. The Abu Dhabi Oil Refining Company is the third-largest domestic petrochemical company after Fertil and Borouge.[10]

To triple the current refining capacity of 485,000 barrels per day, projects such as expanding the existing Ruwais refinery and constructing a new refinery in Fujairah are initiated. These refineries has a strategic opening into the Indian Ocean *vis-à-vis* the choke-point, Strait of Homuz.

The Abu Dhabi National Oil Company has subsidiaries or partnerships in three sovereign wealth funds as Abu Dhabi Inc in upstream and downstream hydrocarbon. As economic national champions, state-owned entities including sovereign wealth funds in Abu Dhabi Inc develop strategic and competitively viable sectors. It is not political to advance national interests, but optimise both commercial and social profit.

One oil sovereign wealth fund is the Abu Dhabi National Energy Company or Taqa PJSC formed in 2005 with 51% owned by the Abu Dhabi Water and Electricity Authority. Taqa's assets include oil drilling in Canada and North Sea and expansions in a European natural-gas storage and power plant. Its Fujairah grassroots export-oriented oil refinery with a capacity of 500,000 barrels per day dwarfs the existing total of 125,000 barrels per day in Ruwais and Umm al-Nar.

Taqa's subsidiary/sovereign wealth fund or investment arm in 1984 is the International Petroleum Investment Company. It goes international into crude oil production, gas pipelines, petrochemicals, oil services, hydrocarbon shipping, hydrocarbon-based power and other hydrocarbon-intensive processing industries, including nitrogenous

---

[9]Producing Borstar enhanced polyethylene which is one among the Borealis specialities, Ruwais is set to become the world's largest ethane manufacturing complex with German engineering Linde Group building an ethane cracker. Borealis processes about 85% of petrochemicals produced by Aktiengesellschaft or OMV, which is Central Europe's biggest oil company. Borealis is the largest customer of OMV refineries in Schwechat and Burghausen, Germany.

[10]It has 60% stake in Abu Dhabi Melamine Industry with Austrian Agroline Melamine International holding 40%, targeting markets in Southeast Asia and China.

fertilisers and aluminium smelting. It first invested in 1988 in a minority of about 9.5% in Spain's second largest refiner/marketer Compañía Española de Petróleos or Cepsa.[11]

The International Petroleum Investment Company has investment of about 50% in Hyundai Oilbank, which is the South Korea's fourth largest refiner and Pak-Arab refinery in Pakistan. With OMV, the International Petroleum Investment Company acquired a majority of about 65% in Borealis[12] by buying a 40% stake in Norway's Statoil. It has expressed interests in Thai, Malaysian, Korean refineries and Royal Dutch Shell's liquefied petroleum gas.[13] It is also considering Nabucco, which is a natural gas pipeline project from Turkey to Europe.

The International Petroleum Investment Company's portfolio was estimated at over $14 billion by 2010[14] in major stakes in 14 world's

---

[11]The International Petroleum Company's decision to increase its stake from 9.5% to 25% was planned, put on hold pending a double taxation agreement between the UAE and Spain which did occur, but the deal was scuttled as the price was deemed too high. It has gone beyond oil like its 4.99% stake in Italy Unicredit for $2.3 billion in 2010.

[12]The International Petroleum Investment Company increased its stake from 25% to 65% while the OMV enhanced its stake to 35% from 25%. OMV's increased share in Borealis via its Abu Dhabi partnerships put its Central European operations and value chain in a better position as integrated with Borealis. OMV also has stakes in the Agroline Melamine International in which the International Petroleum Investment Company put a 50% stake. It is very complex locking-in as Abu Dhabi Melamine Industry 60%-owned by Abu Dhabi Oil Refining Company is also with Agroline Melamine International.

[13]It wanted up to 25% stake in Taiwan's Chinese Petroleum Corporation, but the latter has no plan to privatise, so the two did a feasibility study to jointly invest in a downstream petrochemical facility in Abu Dhabi to manufacture purified terephathalic acid and polyvinyl chloride for plastic items.

[14]International Petroleum Investment Company's $46 billion in international portfolio investment (capital assets and others in equity and money markets) surpassed its $40 billion target before 2013 as the global financial crisis generated investment opportunities. Even earlier in 2006–2008, Aabar Investments acquired Dalma Energy and Pearl Energy. In 2009, with its parent, a 9.1% stake made them the single largest shareholder in Daimler AG, who is the producer of Mercedes-Benz luxury cars and world's largest manufacturer of heavy and medium duty trucks; *The National*, August 5, 2010.

leading hydrocarbon companies including those through its 71% stake in Aabar Investments PJSC, formerly Aabar Petroleum, the third sovereign wealth fund in oil incorporated in 2005[15] with Abu Dhabi Investment Company[16] and Mubadala Development Company, another sovereign wealth fund among its founding investors.

Abu Dhabi as an energy hub seems assured all the way downstream. No matter how low-profiled Abu Dhabi Inc tries to be, both as a producer and by its sizeable and frequent acquisitions in related energy assets, it will inevitably be embroiled in political economy issues of other demandeurs.[17] From Europe and the US to East Asia, all worry about energy security and OPEC supplies.

On gas,[18] anticipating demand since 1999, the UAE Offsets Group and Oman had a memorandum of understanding. The Dolphin

---

[15]Aabar Investments' 2005 flotation created a total capital base of Dh900 million or $245 million. Delisted in 2010 as a PJLC or private PJSC was an option. It deemed market valuation unfair; its shares trade for 20–30% of its book value. A PJLC offers more flexibility to focus on long-term performance, without filing regular earnings reports with much misunderstanding of earnings arising from its complex derivative contracts. After buying out most of Aabar minority shareholders, its parent International Petroleum Investment Company has 86%.

[16]The Abu Dhabi Investment Company as a subsidiary of the Abu Dhabi Investment Authority is distinct from another sovereign wealth fund, the Abu Dhabi Investment Council which is a sister fund to the Abu Dhabi Investment Authority (Chapter 3).

[17]There is much energy tension from the West to East Asia, notably China and Japan all sourcing Arabian Gulf energy; see Emirates Centre for Strategic Studies and Research, ed, 2007a, 2008a, 2008b, 2009a, 2010a; and Taylor, 2007.

[18]With or without any OPEC-like cartel for gas, Van Foreest, 2011 challenges the assumption of natural gas inevitably as the default choice for future power generation, given unrealistically expensive low carbon supply sources comprising renewables, nuclear power and coal with carbon capture and storage on scale necessary to achieve carbon reduction targets in the next decade. Instead, he asks if natural gas needs a decarbonisation strategy to rethink two assumptions; one for a carbon footprint of natural gas and two, how its decarbonisation strategy affects investment for carbon capture and storage, renewable gas and back-up for intermittent renewable energy; http://www.oxfordenergy.org/2011/05/ does-natural-gas-need-a-decarbonisation-strategy-the-cases-of-the-netherlands-and-the-uk/.

pipeline[19] first got to supply refined Omani gas. Another memorandum of understanding with Qatar[20] formed Dolphin Energy as a joint venture for Qatari gas for UAE and Oman. It is the first strategic GCC energy network by Abu Dhabi as an energy niche, possibly extending to Kuwait or Pakistan. A national gas grid as in the electricity grid[21] remains a priority.

Neither the second nor the third Dolphin phase got more gas as Qatar imposed a gas moratorium.[22] A long-term plan to exploit gas[23] once the Abu Dhabi National Oil Company's sole export contract expires in 2019 depends on two gas projects. One is its Shah project separating sulphur from natural sour gas to produce both sulfur and sweet liquefied natural gas. Two is its integrated gas development capturing carbon dioxide from steel and aluminium plants in Mussafah as an alternative gas source.

---

[19]Emiri Decree No 8 of 2002 approved the incorporation of Abu Dhabi-based Dolphin Energy and defined its role. The Supreme Petroleum Council issued its Decision Number 1 of 2002 to clarify corporate, marketing, and distribution details for the Dolphin Energy Ltd. It is owned 51% by the Mubadala Development Company and 24.5% each by Total of France (first international partner in 2000) and Occidental Petroleum of the US which was selected in 2002 after Enron's withdrawal.

[20]While gas-to-liquid technology and other exciting frontiers beckon, Qatargas formed in 1984, pioneered liquefied natural gas as the largest producer in the world of 42 million tonnes per annum in capacity, but has a moratorium to conserve its gas. Some 2 billion cubic feet per day with a line capacity of 3.2 billion cubic feet per day from Qatar's biggest gas at Al Khaleej started in late 2007.

[21]Seven emirate-distributors as one UAE integrated network can deliver five times the gas volumes by Dolphin Energy which caters to 30% of UAE gas consumption.

[22]Qatar's additional, but intermittent gas export is seasonal, depending on short-term domestic demand.

[23]Some old, cheap gas contracts will expire soon, then a gas price shock is anticipated. Compared to what most Abu Dhabi industrial and commercial users paying a subsidised gas price of $1.50 per million British thermal unit, some industrial users in Ras Al Khaimah pay $9 for the same quantum of Dolphin gas. Dubai pays as much as about $20 for the equivalent amount in imports of liquefied gas in 2011 in a deal with Royal Dutch Shell; *The National*, May 24, 2011.

However, a carbon price policy twinning with Masdar renewable energy and carbon capture is yet to evolve.[24] The Abu Dhabi Gas Liquefaction Company has partially decoupled its operations from its oil-producing Abu Dhabi Marine Operating Company for greater flexibility over operations based on Das Island. The Abu Dhabi National Oil Company, its 16 subsidiaries, joint ventures and sovereign wealth funds can change the hydrocarbon landscape, but need a long-term gas plan and policy, hand-in-hand.

2.3. Renewable Energy, Green Technology, and Sustainable Development

The Mubadala Development Company created the Abu Dhabi Future Energy Company or Masdar in 2006. It makes the necessary investment, joined by the Abu Dhabi National Oil Company, Abu Dhabi Water and Electricity Authority, Abu Dhabi Education Council and Environmental Agency Abu Dhabi to oversee, implement, and develop all four Masdar clusters which is hosted in Masdar City as a special economic zone.

The Masdar Initiative is multifaceted comprising the Masdar Institute, Masdar Capital, Masdar Power, Masdar Carbon, and Masdar City to develop and integrate the full renewable and clean technology lifecycle, from research to commercial deployment. It aims to create scalable clean energy solutions with global partners with proven technologies venturing into new research.

The Masdar Institute designed and built by Foster + Partners, in cooperation with the Massachusetts Institute of Technology has graduated its first batch of postgraduate students in 2011.[25] Its

---

[24]Economics is holding up the greenhouse gas capture and storage project by Masdar and Abu Dhabi National Oil Company; *The National*, May 24, 2011.

[25]Anecdotally, of 85 Master's students since 2009, only five are Emiratis and one is proceeding to doctoral. Without bonds to full scholarships, sequestered in dormitories and campus enclaves not assimilated to local work culture and life, many may return home. Employers prefer locals and experienced workers. It suggests a better design for human resources development and deployment.

colossal wind tower as a symbol of its zero-energy concept is a simple modern version of the traditional Arabian cooling system,[26] to be the first of a system of wind towers by 2016. Masdar City is planned as the world's first large-scale carbon-neutral development, housing some 40,000 people. It hosts the headquarters for the International Renewable Energy Agency (IRENA).[27]

Despite known geography, climate, water scarcity and depleted aquifers, new technologies for desalination, renewable energy and solar by the Masdar Institute proved harder than expected. Solar panels, developed by satellite mapping techniques, did not apparently account for dust and humidity factors until the introduction of coatings that enabled photovoltaic panels to improve the capturing capability of the panel. Another form of solar capture by concentrated mirrors also helps.

To improve solar resource maps by remote sensing and modelling, the Masdar Institute took environmental factors into account in big solar plants in the desert or small photovoltaic arrays on city rooftops. The electric grid is to get smarter to handle distribution and intermittent energy supplies. Abu Dhabi's desert, long coastline and salty soils are integrated into seawater agriculture system for aquaculture production of shrimp, fish and even cultivation of salt-tolerant salicornia plant and mangroves.

Salicornia is harvested for oil seed and processed into biofuels. Mangroves need sea water for irrigation, which acts as a beneficial natural treatment system for wastewater from aquaculture ponds, to increase biodiversity and greening the coastline. Masdar projects practise the three R's in environment-friendly reduce, reuse, or recycle as solid and

---

[26]The 45-metre high passive ventilation system is designed to capture the desert's breezes and cool the air in Masdar City by as much as 2°C. Costing $16 billion, down by 27% from the original cost announced in 2008, it is declared like everything else in the green city, an experiment, testing ideas over months or years to change first Masdar Institute and then Masdar City as it expands; *The National*, March 6, 2011.
[27]Abu Dhabi's successful bid for IRENA in 2009 reflects its commitment tap nuclear energy for civilian use. It hosted the first IRENA summit for 139 signatory nations; *Gulf News*, January 17, 2010.

liquid waste turn into fuel and other raw materials. Nanotechnology makes cellulose-based polymers for biodegradable food packaging.

Over time, Masdar Institute has laboratory infrastructure, capability in research and development for innovation, funding, talents, and expertise to develop advanced materials for lighter, safer and more sustainable aircraft, and better ways to design and make microchips for the aerospace and semiconductor sectors. A consistent policy framework for sustainability needs protected intellectual property rights.

Masdar projects include physical economic modelling to investigate the future impact of energy and environmental policy and various studies in innovation dynamics, generation of new clean-tech businesses, climate change, impact on local economy and comparative renewable energy policies in the world. Dare-to-dream lofty goals with a committed leadership, bright minds of dedicated individuals seem to be at work, experimentally to self-sustainable commercialisation.

Masdar Capital has two funds, the Masdar Clean Technology Fund and the Deutche Bank Masdar Clean Tech Fund that were launched in 2006 and 2009, respectively[28] to promote and commercialise renewable technologies. They include clean energy (power generation and storage, transportation, cleantech/clean energy innovation and sustainable biofuels); environmental resources (water and waste management to sustainable agriculture); energy and material efficiency (advanced materials, building and power-grid efficiency and enabling technologies); and technologies in other environmental services.

Masdar Power has a portfolio of renewable power generation projects of $5 billion.[29] Its overseas investment seems more promising, but Masdar is key to delivering at least 7% of Abu Dhabi's power

---

[28] The first is a fully deployed $250 million fund, invested $45 million in three cleantech funds and the rest of $205 million in 12 direct investment in companies as lead or co-lead investor; http://www.masdar.ae.

[29] Masdar Power has three solar projects in Spain worth $1 billion. One 20-megawatt plant produces power since May 2011, another two 50-megawatt facilities in 2011. It has stakes in the one-gigawatt London Array offshore wind farm and six-megawatt offshore wind project Seychelles. Domestic projects include the Shams one project as the largest concentrated solar plant in the Middle East with Abengoa SA, Spain and Total SA, France, 100-megawatt Noor one photovoltaic plant to be contracted by end

from renewable sources by 2020. Growth in power demand is over 20,000 megawatts by the end of the decade to need 1,500 megawatts from various Masdar projects. Since the global financial crisis, some reassessments seem equally pertinent.[30]

Masdar Carbon manages projects for reductions in carbon emissions through energy efficiency, recovery of waste heat/carbon dioxide and by carbon capture and storage under the current UN-based Clean Development Mechanism or other applicable future international climate trading schemes. Carbon emissions are monetised for industrial asset owners in end-to-end solutions, from carbon finance to identify and manage project, technology sourcing project analysis and registration at the UN.

As an exemplary Arab Gulf state,[31] the UAE signed various international agreements with other nuclear states to tap nuclear energy for civilian purposes only. The Federal Authority for Nuclear Regulation and the Emirates Nuclear Energy Corporation as the operator have a team led by the Korea Electric Power Corporation to design, build and help to operate four 1,400-mega-watt nuclear power units.[32]

Sustainable development in the environment or ecology system means no green house gas emission, pollution, or excess waste. Under

---

2011 and building a 30-megawatt wind farm on Sir Bani Yas island. It already operates a 10-megawatt concentrated solar plant reflecting sunlight with mirrors to heat liquids, create steam, turn turbines and generate power; *Bloomberg* and *The National*, May 25, 2011. Its local joint venture with Spain's Sener company is shelving plans for rooftop solar panels. It is no surprise with Abu Dhabi's subsidised utility charges and 80% as expatriates, the majority from South Asia as peripatetic low-cost labour; *The National*, January 1, 2011.

[30]As outlined in a prospectus of a government-guaranteed $1.5 billion bond issued by Waha Aerospace in August 2010 reflecting a series of modifications. For Masdar, its later phases will be postponed as prudent business continues to carefully examine projects without announcing any details.

[31]From Saudi Arabia to Jordan, others are tapping nuclear for energy, green environment and job creation.

[32]The contract for the construction, commissioning and fuel loads for four units was $20 billion, with a high percentage of the contract being offered under a fixed-price arrangement. In addition to the delivery of the four plants, the two UAE agencies and South Korea have also agreed to key terms for Korean investors to have an equity

sustainable economic development, each generation uses the world's resources to satisfy needs and reasonable wants, leaving enough for the next generation. Both imply no destruction of resources or the environment, therefore no global warming.

Preservation of every breed of birds, animals, and plants in Sir Bani Yas island, planting mangroves or putting Bu Tinah to be voted as one of the seven natural wonders of the world in 2010 is more than winning a contest.[33] Equally, preserving 280 species of fish,[34] including 20 fished commercially augmented food supplies. Productivity and yield are up by electronics and computers to track shoals. Subsidies for Al Foah date farm since 2005 has spawn Al Nassma Chocolate and Liwa Date Festival in Al Ain.

More than exporting camel milk, Camel Mazayen is organised annually by the Abu Dhabi Authority for Culture and Heritage at Zayed City in Al Gharbia. Traditional dhow-building *vis-à-vis* a fibre-glass boat is truly a dying trade.[35] Pearl-diving may be relegated to a sport, for tourism, museums or culture to be documented and given voice. Some entrepreneurs can revitalise cottage industries for jobs, especially the one by home-bound female Emiratis, all part of such total sustainable development is by Khalifa Fund.

2.4. Industrialisation as Planned

To link quickly to industrialisation as planned, a few laws include Law No. 10 of 1970, later known as Industry Law, considered the first statutory decree to organise industry (manufacturing in Arabic) in

---

interest in the project. The first of the four units is scheduled to begin providing electricity to the grid in 2017, with the three later units by 2020.

[33] The Environment Agency Abu Dhabi launched a Dh28 million campaign as Bu Tinah emerged as one of the 28 finalists from a list of 447 sites across 224 countries, in the final phase of a global poll to choose the New Seven Wonders of Nature.

[34] The Fisheries Department registered 5,571 fishing boats in 2006, down from 7,681 in 1999. In 2006, 11,780 licensed fishermen operated in 60 fishing cooperatives. The Environment Agency Abu Dhabi is concerned to protect declining stocks by capping fishing licences at 1,100 since 2002.

[35] *The National*, February 27, 2010.

Table 2.2. Government Industrial Corporation/General Holding Company factories.

Factory	Location
Emirates Flour and Animal Feed Factory	Musaffah
Abu Dhabi National Pipes and Bags Factory	Musaffah
Hobas Gulf Factory	Al Mafraq
Concrete Block Factories	Al Wathba, Al-Mafraq and Al-Ain
Emirates Cement Factory	Al-Ain
Al-Ain Coldstores and Ice Factory	Al-Ain
Al-Ain Mineral Water Bottling Factory	Al-Ain
Emirates Iron and Steel Factory	Musaffah
Dubai Cables Ltd Co (Ducab)	Dubai (50:50 owned, Abu Dhabi:Dubai)

Source: Department of Economy.

Abu Dhabi. An Industrial Loan Fund of worth Dh100 million, in 1997, provided credit and loan facilities through the Government Industrial Company as an equity partner and instrumental to set up many government-owned factories (Table 2.2) in various industrial cities.

The Government Industrial Company was cancelled by Law No. 9 of 2001 as the Department of Economy succeeded it. Its industries were transferred to the General Holding Company. Finally, Law No. 3 of 2004 set up the Higher Corporation for Specialised Economic Zones (called Zonescorp in 2006) headquartered in Musaffah with many branches.

Pre-Vision 2030, industrialisation triangulated around first, Zonescorp[36] with the makings of Bedaya as a forerunner of Khalifa

---

[36]Zonescorp's industrialisation plans were done by the Jurong International Consulting (*et al.*, 2004a and 2005) based on Singapore's industrialisation as the basis for setting up in 2004 the Higher Corporation for Specialised Economic Zones. Separately, another plan was by McKinsey and Company also in 2005.

Fund, worker residential cities[37] and Abu Dhabi Basic Industries Corporation. Second is General Holding Company as a business developer (with Abu Dhabi Trade House briefly[38]), privatising and reinvesting in new projects including railway.[39] Third is an infrastructure fund based on public–private partnership of government-owned Abu Dhabi Commercial Bank and Macquarie Bank.

As a precursor to Vision 2030, a verbalised five-point strategy[40] in 2005 includes more privatisation of factories by the General Industrial Corporation, strengthening the Abu Dhabi Stock Market, focusing high-value, capital- and energy-intensive industries,[41] and finally, creation of Zonescorp's specialised economic zones and tourism under the Abu Dhabi Tourism Authority.[42]

Like a jigsaw puzzle of industrialisation, Figs. 2.1, 2.2, 2.3, and 2.4 show the thinking for the Higher Corporation for Specialised Economic Zones based on a cluster-cum-agglomeration approach (Akifumi *et al.*, eds, 2010; Shahid *et al.*, 2008).[43] As appurtenant to the Department of Economic Development, Zonescorp focuses on issuing industrial licenses and managing its industrial estates.

---

[37] See Jurong International Consulting, *et al.*, 2004b.

[38] As recommended by Jurong International Consulting, *et al.*, 2005, pp.105–109, it existed as a joint venture with Marubeni Company since 2007, but folded under the General Holding Company by 2010.

[39] Originally called the Union Railway, Etihad Railway as a special project under the Department of Economic Development will link the whole of UAE to the proposed GCC Railway.

[40] This was in a speech by the then chairman of then Department of Economy, Sheikh Hamad bin Zayed Al Nahyan, at a launch of emerging Abu Dhabi in 2006 with Mubadala Development Company and Oxford Business Group.

[41] As heavy industries are closed down in the US and Europe due to the high costs of production, Abu Dhabi has cost advantages for petrochemical, steel and aluminium plants to meet global demand; *Middle East Economic Digest*, 2010.

[42] Both tourism and airport development were under the then Department of Economy, with its chairman then also chairman of Etihad Airlines in 2009.

[43] An emphasis on innovation is agglomeration due to "lumpy" aggregative effects associated with economies of scale and network externality of information technology beyond clustering.

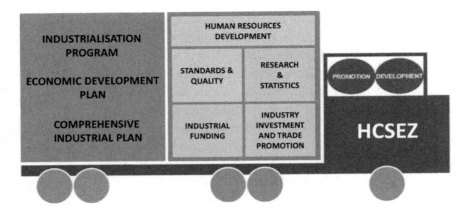

Figure 2.1   Institutional set-up for HCSEZ.

Source: Jurong International Consulting *et al.*, 2005, Book 3, Diagram 4, p. 20.

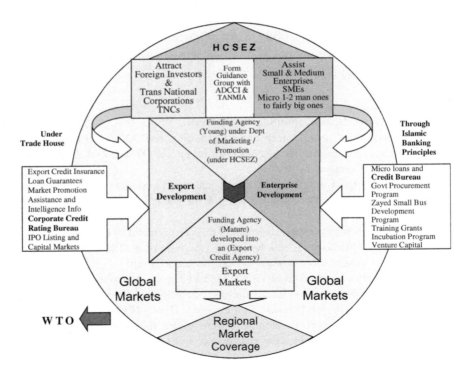

Figure 2.2   Whole industrial financing process.

Source: Jurong International Consulting *et al.*, 2005, Book 3, Diagram 37, p. 256.

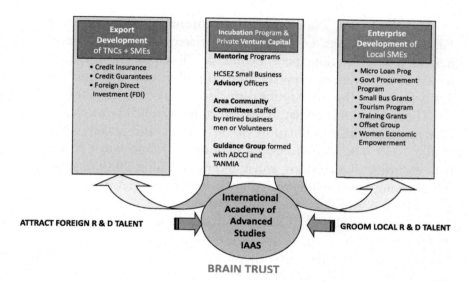

Figure 2.3   The programmes and schemes.

Source: Jurong International Consulting *et al.*, 2005, Book 3, Diagram 38, p. 256.

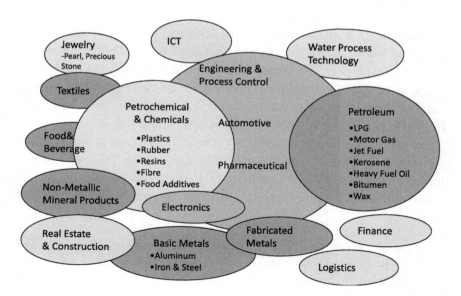

Figure 2.4   Example of a cluster matrix.

Source: Jurong International Consulting *et al.*, 2004, Book 3, Fig. 6.5.1, p. 70.

Much of the Zonescorp's institutional capacity-building in Fig. 2.1 are undertaken by other associated affiliates.[44] There was neither a singular Singapore Economic Development Board nor a whole-of-government from the start to pull in one direction. Figure 2.4 is typical of the 12 manufacturing-service sectors in Vision 2030.

The General Secretariat in the Executive Council remains in overall oversight and coordination of 60 entities and stakeholders for Vision 2030. The Department of Economic Development is charged with ensuring alignment to, and attaining of Vision 2030 targets with other economic stakeholders. It has at least two other plans.

First is a five-year Economic Development Strategic Plan for 2008–2012 introduced in 2009. Ten sectors were selected focussed under this plan — sectors are financial services; building materials; transport and logistics; petrochemicals; tourism; information communication technology; media; oil and gas services; renewable energy; and civil aerospace. The first four sectors account for 75% of Abu Dhabi's GDP to drive the desired incremental growth during the five-year planned period. Compared to the dozen in Vision 2030, healthcare equipment and education are out, but building materials are in.

Based on a bottom-up approach, centred on high-growth non-oil sectors in Vision 2030, the economy-wide plan is in coordination and interaction with over 75 entities. Major gaps are identified in the private sector, small and medium-sized enterprises, employment and regional balance. Challenges are in infrastructure, coordination, and alignment. Tradeoffs include impacts on the environment and population.

In 2011, the Department of Economic Development has another plan for an industrial/manufacturing strategy with the usual stakeholders, plus Abu Dhabi Chamber of Commerce and Industry and Industrialist Union Society.[45] A three-layered level comprises

---

[44]The Department of Economic Development has directorates as International Economic Relations (works-in-progress for export and investment promotion, Sec. 2.5), Studies and Commercial Affairs. It spun off Statistics Centre Abu Dhabi in 2008 and Quality Control Council in 2010.

[45]Maxwell Stamp Plc is the consultant for A Five-year Strategy for the Industrial Sector.

top-down, bottom-up and enterprise based on high economic visibility and alignment to Vision 2030.

The nine sectors are aerospace; construction materials; engineered metal products; food processing; oilfield equipment; packaging; plastics; renewable technologies; transportation equipment based on three existing anchors of petrochemical, steel and aluminium. Not included in Vision 2030, the tenth is semiconductor, *fait accompli* by Mubadala Development Company.

Understandably, Vision 2030's initial dozen sectors are broad guidelines, which are refined by the Department of Economic Development in two sets of 10 focus sectors each. Paralysis of analysis is over fine-tuning. How both sets and plans are put together and aligned to Vision 2030 is another work-in-progress with various enabling agencies, some with very clear mandates of their own as in tourism or aerospace or semiconductor.

There seems to be no value-added except to be truly certain and confident, but at least as timely reiterations of Vision 2030 and incorporating the regional plans by the East Region Development Council and West Region Development Council. The industrial strategy is also a reminder for a review of all laws and regulations (Chapter 4).

2.5. Industrialisation as Practised

The Department of Economic Development seems atop[46] of planned industrialisation in theorising transformation and recording generic outcomes.[47] Spinning off autonomous entities are works-in-progress,[48]

---

[46]By 2011, the same chairman chairs the Department of Economic Development, Abu Dhabi Council for Economic Development and Zonescorp, serving as deputy chair in General Holding Company and on other boards, for better coordination and cooperation.

[47]See Kakabadse *et al.*, 2011 as a roadmap to a world-class government and Department of Economic Development, 2010 profiling Abu Dhabi's *Time to Shine*; http//www.adeconomy.ae.

[48]Reminiscent of earlier studies as in Figs. 2.1 and 2.2, the International Development Ireland Ltd in 2011 is fleshing out the organisation and structure of the Export Promotion Agency and Investment Promotion Agency under the International

including either a traditional export–import bank or an export credit and insurance agency (Fig. 2.2).[49] In practice, other enabling entities are hands-on as project-based to actuate industrialisation in free zones or directly spur big, small, and medium-sized enterprises, start-ups or entrepreneurs.

Variously called special economic zones, export processing zones, even science parks for high-technology industries, free zones basically offer incentives to the investors within a bounded area. In bonded warehouses, industrialists are allowed to import raw materials exempted from customs duties provided that finished products are exported and not sold domestically. They promote exports, usually high value-added with exempted duties or developmental assistance for research and development in science parks.

All free zones in the UAE allow full repatriation of capital as tax havens with 100% foreign ownership of companies and factories versus 49% outside free zones. Freehold land as universally understood is only for Emiratis and the states. Abu Dhabi's 100% ownership for real estate is for structures built above the land as usufruct, suitable as collateral for mortgages and loans. In reality for foreigners they have 99-year leases, renewable another 99-year.[50]

Given special jurisdictional and regulatory powers within the free zones, they are *ultra vires*, which means that they are not subject to the law of the land. Dubai is most agile in creating free zones as a law unto itself to industrialise faster as first-comer advantage.[51]

Economic Relations directorate. It follows Booz & Company's reorganisation report, 2009 for the Department of Economic Development. Legislation for autonomy is time-consuming; *status quo* most likely without change agents.

[49] Ironically, Dubai's Export Credit Insurance Company of the Emirates for all UAE exporters is short of funds; *The National*, April 21, 2011.

[50] They are subject to various property laws of Abu Dhabi and Dubai, with no federal property law as yet.

[51] At present in Dubai, there are 21 existing free zones, such as Jebel Ali Free Zone (Dubai), Dubai Airport Freezone, Dubai Internet City, Dubai Media City, Dubai Auto Zone, Dubai Academic City, Dubai Biotechnology & Research Park, Dubai Flower Centre, Dubai Gold & Diamond Park, Dubai Healthcare City, Dubai International Financial Centre, Dubai Knowledge Village, Dubai Logistics City,

A one-stop-shop concept around an industrial cluster for synergy is clear, but too many zones seem to relegate to speculative real estate play. As real estate values plummeted, Dubai landlords are turning more affordable spaces into incubators for innovative entrepreneurs.

Free zones are differentiated by respective efficiency in management, cost and location. Some in Dubai lock-in tenants as a full one-stop-services menu of fee-based support or outsourcing services *in situ*. Dubai relying on user charges and fees based on real estate could be tricky for firms with affiliates across zones in the same emirate; same issues faced by companies operating across emirates with individual licensing rules.

Any inevitable duplication in emirate-regulated free zones is sorted out by market competition varying across sectors and needs. More mature and integrated Economic Zones World and Nasdaq Dubai have an agreement for equity financing opportunities for companies based in the Jebel Ali Free Zone and their initial public offers to be listed on the Dubai stock exchange.[52]

As relative latecomers, Abu Dhabi's five free zones are Abu Dhabi Ports Company owning Khalifa Port Industrial Zones or Kizad, Abu Dhabi Airport Free Zone, Masdar City, twofour54 and Zonescorp. All are affiliated clusters for synergy and economies of scale and scope with horizontal integration within sectors and vertical integration across sectors.

Abu Dhabi Ports Company established by Emiri decree No. 6 of 2006 is a master developer and regulator of ports and industrial

---

Dubai Maritime City, Dubai Multi Commodity Centre, Dubai Outsource Zone, Dubai Silicon Oasis, Dubai Studio City, Enpark (Dubai), International Media Production Zone (Dubai), International Humanitarian City (Dubai) with six coming up as Dubai Auto Parts City, Dubai Building Materials Zone, Dubai Carpet FZ, Dubai Cars & Automotive Zone, Dubai Textile City and Heavy Equipment & Trucks Zone (Dubai); also Ras Al Khaimah FTZ and RAK Investment Authority, two in Sharjah as Hamriyah Free Zone and Sharjah Airport International, one each Fujairah Free Zone, Ahmed Bin Rashid FZ (Umm Al Quwain) and Ajman Free Zone; see http//www.uaefreezones.ae. and Balakrishnan, *et al.*, eds, 2010 for managing some UAE businesses, including Jebel Ali Free Zone.

[52] *Gulf News*, April 13, 2011,

zones, mainly Kizad in Taweelah. It is mandated to develop all ports (except oil and gas and military ports) and related infrastructure to develop and incubate new firms in its ports and industrial zones. Its Abu Dhabi Terminals is a joint venture with Mubadala Development Company. Industrial licenses for Kizad are issued by Zonescorp. Kizad companies are registered by the Department of Economic Development.

Kizad focuses on advanced industries in aluminium including a fully integrated aluminium smelter[53] by Emirates Aluminium (Emal); engineered metals; steel; petrochemical and chemical; pharmaceutical and healthcare equipment; food; trade, warehousing and logistics. Emal costing $5.7 billion is owned 50% by Mubadala Development Company and 50% by Dubai Aluminium (Dubal) since 2007. This leads to a ratio of 50:50.

Situated half way between Abu Dhabi and Dubai, the largest green-field Emal smelter replicates Ducab in the ratio of 50:50 (Table 2.2). The first phase of the Emal (aluminium complex) in 2009 is followed by a second 6-square kilometre site. The large space was expected to double the production capacity of 750,000 tonnes of aluminium to 1.5 million tonnes annually.

Focused vertically integrated clusters with related midstream and downstream processes are supported by other suppliers and service providers in a value chain. Anchor tenants produce basic materials and mid-stream producers take them as feedstock to produce value-added products. Finally, downstream producers produce finished goods to add more value to the derived product.

Warehousing and logistics facilities are available for firms to distribute and export the goods. A Hot Metal Road is specially constructed to transport and deliver molten aluminium, saving downstream manufacturers the cost of re-melting ingots. Production of aluminium is energy-intense consuming 15,000 kilowatts per tonne (of aluminium) which is equivalent to 30% of total production cost.

---

[53]The 40-year old integrated Bahrain Aluminum is a template with downstream extrusion plant, rolling mill and cable plants.

Tacaamol is the Taweelah petrochemical complex to be onstream in 2014 for 10 million tonne per year in capacity as part of a new polymer park by Abu Dhabi National Chemicals Company or Chemaweyaat. A deficit of ethane as a traditional feedstock[54] may have feedstock from Dolphin Energy on a 25–30 year gas supply contract. Kizad's on-site power station complex is run by the Abu Dhabi Water and Electricity Authority.

Abu Dhabi Airport Free Zone incorporated by Emiri decree No. 5 of 2006 is the owner and operator of Abu Dhabi International Airport. It is establishing a business and logistics park dubbed under Sky City to generate non-aeronautical revenue to finance airport development with less reliance on state grants. Near to the Abu Dhabi International Airport is Masdar City.

Media Zone Authority was established by Law No.12 of 2007 with twofour54 (Abu Dhabi's coordinates) or Media City as a free trade zone, tax-free and 100% foreign ownership for the development of world class Arabic media and entertainment organisations. Its main policy was "by Arab for Arab".

It comprises three key pillars: twofour54 tadreeb (training academy in 2011 acquired Dubai business of SAE Institute world's largest network of media training academies), twofour54 ibtikar (innovation and support) and twofour54 intaj (state-of-the-art production facilities). All are supported by business enabler twofour54 tawasol (one-stop-shop). Tenants in twofour54 have a choice of telecommunication operators.[55]

Some free zones may have a conflict of interest that arises as owner-regulator-operator. A lesson is how the Telecommunications Regulatory Authority is separated from its operators, etisalat and du.

---

[54] Alternative feedstock as more versatile exists with trade-offs. Naphtha or natural gas liquids mean lower rates of returns, but more job opportunities are created from a wider range of products. Smaller but more stable revenue streams are from co-products, specialty chemicals, aromatics and intermediate petrochemicals. Saudi Aramco's proposed joint venture with Dow Chemicals uses a mixture of ethane and propane rather than pure naphtha-based.

[55] twofour54 is the first Abu Dhabi free zone to have a choice from a duopoly of operators, of "etisalat" or "du"; *The National*, April 5, 2011.

This three-in-one conflict is realised and being tackled in Zonescorp. Uniform licensing of Zonescorp and Kizad tenants is right by the Department of Economic Development as Abu Dhabi and Dubai duo competes globally.

The pair of Zonescorp and Kizad is more than any *prima facie* rivalry to launch projects. They are collaborating in a new set of industrial cities in building materials city, metals city, polymer park and oil and gas city in parallel with other services cities (Chapter 3). Zonescorp's automotive industry zone as a centre for vehicle assembly, services and sales is a new cluster in 11-square kilometre city in Musaffah.[56]

The pioneer Industrial City of Abu Dhabi attracted an investment of Dh6 billion for 200 industrial ventures (http//www.zonescorp. com). Its first extension, from 14-square kilometre by another 10-square kilometre, financed by the Infrastructural Fund, led to a $400 million second Industrial City of Abu Dhabi in 2005. This is a mixed industrial zone, from basic metals to paper and wood products with two public–private partnership clusters for building and construction materials; and oil and gas services.

A third Dh600 million Industrial City of Abu Dhabi provides more basic above-the-ground industrial infrastructure like road network and utilities. It has a Dh360 million affluent plant project with a capacity to treat 80,000 cubic metres of industrial sewer daily. The treated water obtained from the such a treatment plant is recycled and used for landscaping. A fourth Industrial City of Abu Dhabi as 34-square kilometre for metal, building materials, logistics and oil and gas, and a fifth to meet rising demand for industrial land are planned.

The Abu Dhabi Ports Company's new Khalifa Port is a shift away from Port Zayed.[57] Also as a result of new Khalifa Port, the proposed port for Mussafah is scrapped. Further, Kizad and Zonescorp would be

---

[56]Aldar Properties' one-stop MotorWorld is for car sales in Shamkah near Abu Dhabi International Airport. Zonescorp has a second-hand car sales centre. Such land-intensive facilities are relocated from the city.

[57]The port, Mina Zayed area will be redeveloped into a commercial and cruise hub.

linked by railway instead. Taweelah's 100-square kilometre upgradeable to 480-square kilometre is a 50-year project for transshipment, industrial and commercial zones and logistics hub. Khalifa Port would ramp up from 33 million tonnes to 80 million tonnes for bulk and general cargo.

Abu Dhabi Executive Council encourages broader scope on multi-sectoral projects beyond manufacturing that are modelled as public–private partnerships. More intra- and inter-emirate cooperation spreads industrialisation faster; Abu Dhabi to Dubai and Zonescorp to Kizad, respectively. Dubai's Jebel Ali Free Zone is running out of space. Opportunities beckon to complement and supplement. Abu Dhabi and Dubai encompass Kizad-Zonescorp-Emal-Dubal that even includes Dubai's infrastructure.

These ambitious scales however, have been checkmated by the global financial crisis, affecting the $10 billion Shah sour gas project, Masdar Initiative and Kizad. Abu Dhabi's traditional lump sum contract was changed to design-and-build with timely fresh prices for a reduced scope of work to reap falling cost since the global recession.[58] It is a blessing in disguise in raising cooperation and sobering grand scales.

A second pair of big industrial players comprises the General Holding Company PJSC and Abu Dhabi Basic Industries Corporation.[59] The former was set up by Law No. 5 of 2004. It owns the latter, formed in 2007, specifically for industrial development and investment. Both with Zonescorp and the infrastructure fund are part of the triangulation or family. The General Holding Company's four-pronged strategy is to create, develop, privatise, and reinvest in business in Abu Dhabi.

After partially privatising Agathia and Al Foah in 2004, General Holding Company's Dh 857.5 million initial public offer of three cement factories, the Emirates Cement Factory of Al Ain and Emirates

---

[58]The original contract involves onshore port facilities, 47 buildings including the largest for central facilities and all works to complete by 2011; see *Middle East Economic Digest*, May 7–13, 2010.

[59]The relationship between the two is circuitous with the chairman of Abu Dhabi Basic Industries Corporation also the vice-chairman of General Holding Company.

Concrete Block Factories of Al Ain and Mafraq in 2006 actually raised capital for expansion into a fully-integrated plant.[60] It is modest in assets (Table 2.2) unlike Mubadala Development Company, but both have a social role.

General Holding Company's priority is to expand the private sector in domestic development by forming strategic public–private partnerships favouring privatisation. It inculcates an equity stakeholder culture. Its philosophy is for a series of projects for the private sector with only a small, minimum shareholding by the state. Its first 2009 earnings report is a part of a transparency policy following the annual reports of the Abu Dhabi Investment Authority and Mubadala Development Company.[61]

It focuses on the basic metals such as aluminium, steel and copper, also petrochemical and other industrial sectors. Its flagship is Emirates Steel Industries, a growing subsidiary from a simple steel processor, to become the largest UAE integrated steel plant. The General Holding Company is not privatising Emirates Steel Industries. It is moving its $1 billion planned steel plate production project from Taweelah to Musaffah, Western Region or Ruwais for reasons from logistics to integration and most of all, job creation and more even regional development.[62]

A third big industrial force is the sovereign wealth funds beside the above oil funds. A three-in-one case-study is highlighted to show

---

[60] A new company called the Arkan Building Materials Company was created by merging Al Ain Cement Factory and two concrete block companies.

[61] General Holding Company's net profit rose by 61% that amounts to Dh1.13 billion in 2009 from Dh703 million in 2008, profit grew by 454% in five years to Dh1.13 billion from Dh204 million in 2004 (the compound annual growth rate is 40.83%). It plans to invest $10 billion over the next five year in petrochemical, metal and others. Having grown by more than Dh15 billion over five-year period, it reckons that it has added over 13% to Abu Dhabi's non-hydrocarbon industrial GDP with a workforce of over 17,000; *Khaleej Times*, May 10, 2010.

[62] Also, Emirates Steel Industries lost its bid to acquire Oman's Shadeed Iron and Steel as Abu Dhabi-owned Al-Ghaith Holdings sold it to India's Jindal. Comparatively, by capacities in million tonnes per year Shadeed is 1.5, Bahrain's Hidd steel mill is 4, Saudi Jizan steel plan is 1.5 and Emirates Steel Industries by phase 3 is 1.4.

their strategic intent in economic development and outcome for Vision 2030. The first is the UAE Offsets Group[63] which owns the second, Mubadala Development Company which in turn owns the third, Advanced Technology Investment Company. They share a similar philosophy as a team.

The UAE Offsets Group facilitates partnerships between international business and local entrepreneurs since its inception in 1992. The UAE had a unique situation after the Gulf war to procure a large amount of equipment to modernise its armed forces and maintain its safety and security vantage.

In the UAE Offsets Group programme, all contractors must form a joint venture in the UAE with local partners. The contractor, not bureaucrats, decides on the joint venture's activity and technology. Offsets credit is not given up-front as in other countries, only from profitable performing companies, up to 60% of contract value over an average duration of seven years.

The privatisation trend via initial public offer is an opportunity for the UAE Offsets Group as other venture funds face bureaucratic red tape and risks, with laws not fully developed. Two missing dots remain, namely, monitor offsets credit with auditing and risk management and offsets credit for training in profitable companies. Non-profitable training can be a part of the government's responsibility.

---

[63]When a foreign company is awarded a large government defence contract, it is contractually obliged to contribute economic activity to the local economy to partially offset the negative effect of such expenditure going abroad. Offsets often involve technology transfer, technical training, more business opportunities, joint ventures and in some cases, the creation of entire industries. Over 80 nations have some form of offsets. Every major defense contractor is involved in various offsets forms like regional benefits, licensing, co-production, localisation, barter, countertrade and such. Offsets programmes have evolved from direct procurement of the specific technology to indirect dealing with large global companies. Offsets credit may be given, but there may be no substance behind it as the rule, leading to litigation and bureaucrat legions formed to monitor offsets and their fulfillment. Both the General Agreement on Tariffs and Trade (GATT) and WTO have banned offsets as discriminatory unless countries seek exceptions on security and technology grounds.

The UAE Offsets Group's joint ventures are varied. They include Abu Dhabi Shipbuilding, a collaboration with Newport New Ship Yards, the largest ship yard in the world; the National Science and Technology Institute, a collaboration with Bechtel, the world largest contract research company; Gulf Energy Systems in alliance with Duke University and others; Gulf Diagnostic Centre; Combined Cargo UAE; and others in district cooling, agriculture, waste management and aircraft leasing.

A new shipping company, Gulf Energy Maritime is a joint venture involving Abu Dhabi's International Petroleum Investment Company, Dubai's Emirates National Oil Company, Oman Oil Company and Thales, an international electronics and systems group. For defence against contractors with smaller obligations, the UAE Offsets Group has set up the Alfiah Fund as an investment vehicle for them to invest in, rather than have to set up independent offsets projects and get credits based on fund performance.

The UAE Offsets Group's subsidiary Mubadala Development Company formed under Emiri Decree No. 12 of 2002 is pivotal in Abu Dhabi's diversification and transformation in Vision 2030. It is the third largest Abu Dhabi wholly government-owned investment vehicle or sovereign wealth fund after Abu Dhabi Investment Authority and International Petroleum Investment Company.

By its ability to form new companies or acquire local and foreign[64] stakes in existing ones in a wide range of sectors such as energy, utility, basic industries, aerospace, electronics and services, Mubadala Development Company spearheads Abu Dhabi into high-technology and high value-added growth. Its first public–private partnership was the UAE University expansion in Al Ain versus its 51% stake in intra-GCC Dolphin Energy.

Starting in 2004, Mubadala Development Company has a 25% stake in the Dutch fleet management giant LeasePlan Corporation

---

[64]It is considering some $13 billion in investment in Brazil in oil and gas, aluminium, semiconductors, infrastructure, aerospace, agribusiness; *The National*, May 24, 2011.

alongside the Volkswagen Group.[65] It has shares in the Aldar Real Estate Services, National District Cooling Company (Tabreed) and Abu Dhabi Shipbuilding. Its venture into global leasing, industrial leasing, financing options for infrastructure, transport and power companies is a part of Abu Dhabi Inc as government strategic interest to access regional and global markets via joint ventures.

Mubadala Development Company acquired 5% or 114 million euro of Ferrari from Italian bank Mediobanca. With above 10% internal rate of return, the investment meets with the Abu Dhabi strategy to bond with global brands. The Ferrari alliance gave birth to the Ferrari theme park for road and racing car testing, professional driving schools to leverage opportunities around brand experiences and merchandising.

With a double bottomline of economic-social profit, beyond petrodollar recycling, technology transfer and skill management, the first grand prix on Yas Island in 2009 was a testimony. There even exists a new cluster of activities that hosts sporting events for products and services, especially tourism. Yas Island's $40 billion in infrastructure has set a standard, considered as template and test-bed, for Abu Dhabi's urban future, efficiency and lifestyles.

Mubadala Development Company has appointed the Aldar Properties as its project manager for the construction of the Imperial College London Diabetes Centre building in Abu Dhabi on a turnkey basis with a 15-year lease agreement between the London Imperial Diabetes Centre and Aldar Properties. All the entities described are part of Abu Dhabi Inc, tribal capitalism as synergy is vital, critical, and inter-agency.

A diverse blend of creative strategic diversification by Mubadala Development Company is clear from its key investment, that comprises: **Abu Dhabi Ship Building**, 40%; **Aldar Properties PJSC**, 7%; **Combined Cargo UAE**, 32.9%; **Dolphin Energy Limited**, 51%,

---

[65]Talks in 2004 failed to make Mubadala Development Company the largest shareholder in Volkswagen, but Mubadala Development Company in Leaseplan acquisition paved the way for Volkswagen to contemplate setting up component and truck factories in the Zonescorp automotive industrial city.

inherited from UAE Offsets Group in 2002, accounts for 80% of revenue; **Horizon International Flight Academy** 100%; **Imperial College London Diabetes Centre** (100%), **Injazat Data Systems,** 60%; **LeasePlan Corporation,** 25%; **National Central Cooling Company or Tabreed,** 5%; **UAE University public-private partnership;** and **Ferrari,** 5%. Its latest is a $4 billion aluminium plant mooted with 1Malaysia Development in Sarawak, East Malaysia.[66]

In 2009, Mubadala Development Company offered $1.75 billion in bonds to international investors, days after its first annual report disclosed a loss.[67] It signifies a shift in gear given the global economic recession after high-profile investment. Its business-building mode makes a compelling case to its sole shareholder as fitting Vision 2030 to diversify and create jobs by relying on self-funding.

In 2010, another new firm Sanad Aero Solutions provided financing and logistical support for airlines to purchase and manage engines and other components. It added one more layer to Mubadala Development Company's aerospace strategy. This included manufacturing composite aircraft parts for Boeing and Airbus in the Al Ain aerospace cluster that planned to build aircrafts by 2018.

Mubadala Development Company's joint venture with Rolls-Royce was called off in 2010. Their initial plan in 2009 was to invest jointly in a new firm in Abu Dhabi to service and repair Rolls-Royce's Trent family of aircraft engines. With Rolls-Royce technology transfer and licensing agreements, a partnership with General Electric would have repair work in engines of several Boeing models in Abu Dhabi by 2013.

A major stake in Advanced Micro Devices, US chipmaker and a financial venture with General Electric would pay off in longer-term

---

[66] *The National,* June 19, 2011.

[67] With a Dh12 billion loss due to write-down of asset value, not sales, the bond offer included $1.25 billion five-year bonds, likely to pay an interest rate of 3.95% points over the rate of five-year US treasury bonds and $500 million 10-year bonds at 462.5 basis points over US treasuries to translate into an interest rate of 6.2% on its five-year bonds. See also interview with its chief operating officer, *The National,* April 30, 2009.

profitability. In 2006, **Mubadala Development Company planned** a plant in Saratoga, New York state. It raised its stake in Advanced Micro Devices in 2007 to 20%. In 2008, it spun off a chip manufacturing system to its majority-owned Advanced Technology Investment Company. After that in 2009, it formed Globalfoundries semiconductor manufacturing company.

Another piece of the jig-saw puzzle fell into place opportunistically. In 2009, the Advanced Technology Investment Company paid $1.8 billion (including debt and convertible preference shares, total deal $3.9 billion) for a majority stake in Chartered Semiconductor Manufacturing (producers of domestic and industrial semiconductors since 1987), Singapore. The acquired Singapore semiconductor plant as the world's third-largest brings some 150 customers.

With new investment of $2 to $3 billion in 2010 to expand operational facilities in Dresden, Singapore, new plants in Saratoga, 2012 and Abu Dhabi, 2015, Globalfoundries has patient money and diverse global-continental reach-cum-supply. It is the world's second-largest producer of customised computer chips by 2009, with a market share of 16.7%. Taiwan[68] leads at 47.7% due to Taiwanese scale economies.[69]

Advanced Technology Investment Company's stake in Globalfoundries rises from 66% in 2009, 87% in 2010 to 91% by end 2011 and finally 100% by early 2012.[70] In 2011, Advanced Micro Device launched its new microprocessor code-named Llano 32 nm Fusion Accelerated Processing Unit to enhance computer user experience, battery life, discrete-level graphics capabilities aimed at desktop and laptop computers rather than smartphones.[71]

[68]Taiwan Semiconductor Manufacturing Company founded in 1987 is in Taiwan's Hsinchu Science and Industrial Park with a market share of 49%, annual sale of $9.83 billion in 2007 and 20,000 employees worldwide. Together with United Microelectronics Corporation, Taiwan is the global industry leader.
[69]*The National*, December 20, 2009.
[70]*Ibid.*, May 18, 2011 and February 5, 2012.
[71]*Marketwire*, May 18, 2011 and http://www.advancedtechlogogyic.com.

Khalifa Fund, formed in 2007, is a key enabler with other aspects of emiratisation (Chapter 4) for small and medium-sized enterprises, entrepreneurship and emiratisation, especially home-bound women, those with special needs and rehabilitating inmates. In supporting industry and supply chain as one of Porter's five-forces, Khalifa Fund[72] as a part of the double-bottomline philosophy has Zonescorp offering its start-ups a 25% discount on the market price of land.

2.6. Science, Technology and Innovation

Connecting the dots for a sustainable development model toward Vision 2030, a Science, Technology and Innovation Policy by the Technology Development Committee was approved by the Executive Council in 2011. Unsurprisingly, with nine other stakeholders, its five elements identified with set milestones are human capital; research and development; enterprise development; infrastructure; and laws and regulations.

The role of Advanced Technology Investment and Abu Dhabi Education Council in science, technology, engineering, and mathematics abbreviated as "stem" is refreshing. Technology innovation centres as goal-oriented are dedicated to five sectors in oil and gas; aerospace; semiconductor; information communication technology; and cleantech in renewable energy and environmental technologies, incorporating areas in education, health, and national security.

Innovation emphasised as an additional stage to Porter's three-stages (Fig. 1.1) is defined by the Technology Development Committee as the introduction of novelty to a process of production, a product or service, or a technology in both, government or business, thus generating sustainable economic or societal value. More than science in laboratories, building capabilities is a right ecosystem with intellectual property rights.

Ambitious targets include a knowledge-based workforce of 100,000 by 2030 needing an increase of 23,000 Emiratis and 46,000 expatriates entering the sector. More than 100 patents granted yearly

---

[72]Its loan value in early 2011 is Dh424.5 million with 222 projects approved, 2,027 trained and 5,339 applications reviewed.

by 2030 is up from nine patents as currently. Revenue of small and medium-sized enterprises is to grow by $4.1 billion from 2010 to 2030, at a compound annual rate of 14.4%.

Big firms with more than 250 full-time employees would generate $13.1 billion, growing yearly by 9.8%. Many new big firms would bring $15.5 billion in annual GDP, hiring over 48,000 more workers with 1,700 new small and medium-sized enterprises producing more than $4.4 billion in GDP, employing 25% of the new workforce.

Gross research and development expenditure as a ratio of GDP, mainly by the government, at 0.05% in 2010 plus 0.01% by business adds 0.06%, rising to 0.75%, 0.82% and 1.57%, respectively in 2030 has business leading. Research scientists and engineers per 1,000 population is 9 in 2010 with room to grow to Norway' 10, South Korea's 9.7, Singapore's 9.3 and the US' 9.2.

The UAE's ranking as 22 out of 125 in the International Intellectual Property Rights Index in 2010 seems respectable as a consumer society. But multinational corporations need protected, enforced patents, copyrights and trademarks to be confident to relocate creative research to Abu Dhabi. Equally hard are laws and regulations to improve in the World Bank's doing business survey, the education-cum-manpower plan with a "stem" culture for Emiratis, and a calculated immigration policy.

The Petroleum Institute, Masdar Institute, Emirates Nuclear Energy Corporation, Federal Authority for Nuclear Regulation, armed forces and other professional bodies need to come together with recharged universities. There is no science park except for some perfunctory laboratories, more as pure real estate facilities. A military-defence complex seems to be in the making by UAE Offsets Group and related sovereign wealth funds.

A distinction between technoglobalism and technonationalism is noted. The former is a strong interaction between the internationalisation of technology and the globalisation of the economy (Turner, ed, 2010). It is a creation of wider cross-border interdependence between individual technology-based firms and economic sectors. It implies an ideal tapping of research and development via global resources in chains and networks of multinational corporations.

In reality, technonationalism prevails for two reasons. One is the true and ultimate ownership of multinational corporations and their technology in home nations. Two is a national science and technology plan in strategic research and development that has immense defence and national security implications. Industrial espionage, national security protection and other political economy issues are sensitive, distinct from innocuous generic science and technology transfer.

Often, research and development stops short at development for many reasons. One is the gap in science and technology resources ranging from human to infrastructure and finance for pioneer research. Two is multinational corporations transfer technology mainly to develop, adapt, and customise products for local markets. This way they leave their pure frontier research at home with intellectual property rights and security.[73]

Abu Dhabi's acquisition of branded global firms for technology upgrading needs to harness the multiplier effects to absorb and diffuse technology[74] more than financial returns. Technology diffusion from big local enterprises and multinational corporations needs a productivity board, especially for small and medium-sized enterprises. Khalifa Fund stops short of that to mine the supply chain for technology transfer and diffusion.

Three additional lessons are noted for technology transplants. Singapore has joint government-business training centres on a 50:50 cost-sharing basis tapping bigger firms, both local and foreign corporate training programmes, aiming to enlarge the pool of generic skills, experiential learning and on-the-job-training. This idea dovetails with the UAE Higher Colleges of Technology's Centres for Excellence for

---

[73]Many Asian national innovation systems including China use strong tactics to ensure true technology transfer with national capabilities to absorb, digest and leapfrog ahead. Singapore's global talent policy is for a vibrant, dynamic lifestyle befitting a state-driven science and technology plan, Biopolis and Fusionpolis.

[74]A distinction between backward (more of the same in output) and forward (upgrading in technology and skill as output expands) linkages for the cluster approach to industrialisation and service growth to harvest technology transfer and learning effects.

Applied Research and Training, in-between a science park and incubator for creative innovation.

Two is having the multinational corporations, especially to train and mentor their outsourcing partners as local small and medium-sized enterprises. It is not pure altruism as quality components done to the required specifications are imperative for final products as competitive and worthy of their brands. It is part of effective supply chain management as one of Porter's five-forces (Fig. 1.2).

Three is another gap to be bridged in a buddy system. Some Emiratis seem to feel disenfranchised relative to the attention for foreign investors and multinational corporations. This is more the pity as Abu Dhabi is not short of funds to assist all parties to upgrade together. More and better communication augmented by project-based learning and training can improve the local private sector's receptivity to technology transfer and diffusion. The Khalifa Fund can value-add in such strategic alliances.

Basic economics of direct foreign investment and multinational corporations is a reality (Shujiro, *et al.*, eds, 2006; Palacious, ed, 2009) to be explained in synchrony with emiratisation. Fear of exploitation as post-colonial imperialism or dominance as already evidenced in labour is neither unreasonable nor illogical. Bringing views and perceptions into the 21st century and Vision 2030 cannot be ignored. Neither can domestic stakeholders be placated by financial support without a true marriage.

Naturally, more traditional, conservative and standalone local enterprises which take pride in their heritage and corporate independence are reserved and careful to new technology including management. They are as mindful of, as they are fearful of the good, bad and ugly of globalisation.

They cannot be left behind on their own if Vision 2030 is to be a rising tide of a private sector lifting all boats. Cultural sensitivity and a more nuanced approach must prevail in a tripartite Abu Dhabi Inc as state, multinational corporations and local firms.

A positive message comes from studies of entrepreneurship (Lee, *et al.*, 1990; Low, *et al.*, 1993; Low, 2005). They invariable show that many local enterprises and small and medium-sized enterprises start as a component and service providers for outsourcing graduate into multinational corporations in their own right.

Appropriate learning by technology transfer and diffusion lead to further reinvention and innovations to suit local conditions. Sophisticated Islamic or green products can tap a growing regional market as a start. It is as uniquely comforting that Abu Dhabi is not fearful of job loss from outsourcing as in the West where relocations to China as the factory-of-the-world has creatively destroyed local jobs.

If it helps Abu Dhabi to wean and prune some low-skilled migrant labour as Emiratis upgrade to labour-saving and high technology jobs, all the better for value adding. In turn, low-cost and labour-intensive work outsourced to workers in their home countries would mean work-to-workers rather than workers-to-work as now, causing security and national identity issues for Emiratis.

Abu Dhabi realises that pure rentier income from hydrocarbon and a passive consumer society must reengineer to a producer economy in globalised, competitive value and supply chains. All the right elements in science, technology and innovation are identified, but translating them into action is not a strong suit. Also, abundant financing is not a substitute for political will and commitment plus a national innovation system including a culture for commercialisation[75] and manpower planning.

2.7. Manpower-Cum-Education Planning

The Technology Development Committee and its stakeholders are in the right direction, with targets and milestone imaging a manpower-cum-education plan. With more from the Abu Dhabi Education Council and a population policy (Chapter 4), a few broad observations of human capital planning are relevant. All identified targets

---

[75]The race to produce the Gulf's first microprocessing chip is between the UAE University in Al Ain as first to pass and American University of Sharjah with SenseHerea company as the first to profit from the technology; see *The National*, May 19, 2011.

need the right force to sculpt the right manpower pyramid as a function of both the industrial structure and demography.

Manpower planning has to be hand-in-hand with education planning, once the missing population-immigration policy is set. In theory, armed with statistics, information, forecasting methodologies and techniques, a crude methodology of a demand approach to education and manpower planning has a few deceptively simple steps. A demand-based plan starts with some projected GDP growth over a planned period, in this case Vision 2030 targets.

This in turn needs an econometric model to project the desired and sustainable GDP growth rates. Again, the Department of Economic Development has built its main macroeconomic model and satellite computable general equilibrium models. The overall GDP growth is then recast or distributed as sectoral GDP growth including productivity growth by sectors.

From these sectoral estimates, their manpower requirements are then mapped out at three levels such as professional and managerial as high skilled; semi-professional as in technicians and technologists as semi-skilled; and finally from production to manual workers as less skilled or unskilled. After that, the current levels of employment by these three skills categories and occupations are projected by the labour force surveys of Statistics Centre Abu Dhabi.

These projections are based on the forecast sector's growth and productivity levels. For example, if manufacturing sector has a target growth rate and productivity level, the number of engineers by detailed categorisation from mechanical to civil engineers, can be estimated for the planned period, with inflow and outflow of migrants.

Once the demand side is forecasted, the supply side to meet demand is from two sources, namely domestic and immigration of foreign workers. The manpower plan doubles as an education plan to make intake projections based on local population growth and cohort of school-leavers. In contrast to *laissez-faire* enrolment policy where students qualify for subjects they choose, student intakes are based on the manpower plan for skills and occupations into universities and the Higher Colleges of Technology.

This is neither simple nor easy as a market-based approach intrudes into freedom and privacy of choices, but misguided choice of disciplines and subjects especially without much career guidance and counselling have proven as painful as now. Three points need to be borne in mind. One is that there is a gestation period as it takes time for the graduates to be ready for employment, including failures and retrying.

Two is the attrition[76] or drop-out rate of students who fail to graduate in the disciple or subject as planned including changing then along the way. Even after graduation, some may change their disciplines and occupations as when an engineering graduate becomes a manager rather than a practicing engineer. Most engineers prefer management jobs, especially when they complete a Master's in Business Administration. Attrition is also caused by migration, probably which is not a problem for Abu Dhabi.

Three is Abu Dhabi has a young, but small Emirati population. Its colleges and universities have a small base to recruit students, often filling up a critical mass with foreign students. This is not necessarily wrong. A more concerted policy to tap foreign talent educated and trained in Abu Dhabi at considerable expense to contribute back as gainfully employed in the new knowledge-based sectors is preferable.

This can be augmented by encouraging the second generation of migrant residents to enrol for graduate ad postgraduate degrees, diplomas and certificates. It helps tertiary institutions short of students. It becomes a consciously upgrading policy for a skilled-intensive labour pool. More of the same humanitarian policy for extended family and dependents is quantity, not quality. A virtue is made of a necessity via a manpower plan.

Manpower plans elsewhere tap immigration as a flexible policy to manage critical shortages. Abu Dhabi is passive without immigration

---

[76]The Singapore attrition rate for engineers is high, at 20% and enrolment at universities and polytechnics is inflated by that factor to reach the desired target. It has certain targets of a manpower pyramid in terms of the high, medium, and low skill composition to suit its industrial structure.

as a valve, but a free flow to 80% migrants as default policy. Issues of cost of training, poaching, short-term labour and residency visas and others (Chapter 4) are magnified in terms of both quantum and complexity.

A selective migration policy based on skills and other criteria with a transparent merit system is not new in Singapore. It has bonds for different periods of human resources development and training, unlike no strings attached scholarships by Abu Dhabi for foreign students. It may be too much economism in the Singapore way, but it is a small open economy without resources as any fallback, except be competitive.

A couple of caveats are noted. One is manpower-cum-education planning is an art, not an exact science. Some crude numbers matching Vision 2030 is better than a *laissez-faire* immigration policy. Two is hard choices need strong rethinking by politicians and policies by technocrats. These are bureaucrats with professional qualifications and skills which are more than administrative efficiency and proficiency.

Given Vision 2030, technocrats with engineering or science and technology background would know and understand industries and their technical needs. They are eminently suited to craft and execute policies and regulations once their political masters have set the direction and path. In the final analysis, they plan a mind-mapping with many pathways and related areas. A holistic, integrated and systemic approach as strategic, pragmatic and open-minded, yet sufficiently firm and consistent is complicated.

Chapter 3

NON-OIL KNOWLEDGE-BASED ECONOMY SERVICES

3.1. Introduction

Having defined and delineated Abu Dhabi's primary and secondary sectors, the residual is non-oil knowledge-based economy services, which is progressively converging into manufacturing-cum-services.[1] It has many industrial plans, but no services plan or better yet, a master operational plan of both for Vision 2030.

The science, technology and innovation policy in five sectors is a useful starting point for an action plan. It links into this chapter which focuses on knowledge-based services (Table 2.1). It *inter alia* explores capital as a conduit for technology transfer and deepening capital formation beyond assets in real estate.

Domestic capital, direct foreign investment for technology, public–private partnerships, privatising state-owned entities and sovereign wealth funds all are meant for the economic development. More than monetising oil wealth sustainably, knowledge services have

---

[1]The US federal agency International Trade Commission found that 39% jobs supported by goods exports are actually in service firms. It concludes that government export promotion creates service-sector jobs, appositely concludes that promoting efficiency in domestic service sector is one of the best ways to boost exports. This implies that service-sector exports are the most promising, including contributions to balance of payments as fees for intellectual property and others; *Financial Times*, August 15, 2010.

a life of their own as an innovation (Fig. 1.1) for the growth of private sector.

Services are deemed less exportable with lower productivity as naturally labour-intensive are less amenable to automation, mechanisation, and robotisation. Technology and outsourcing have enabled services to overcome some handicaps; witness India's exponential growth leapfrogging classical primary, secondary and tertiary stages (Ghani *et al.*, eds, 2010, Ghani, *et al.*, 2011; Daniels *et al.*, eds, 2007). Intangible, over-the-wire digitised services under the General Agreement on Trade in Services (GATS) are more complex than trade in goods under WTO.

Services are traded in four modes. Mode 1 is cross-border trade in the delivery of a service from one country into Abu Dhabi. Mode 2 is consumption abroad by foreign tourists in Abu Dhabi's hotel and hospitality services. Mode 3 is a commercial presence in banking services provided by a foreign bank as a service supplier in Abu Dhabi and foreign direct investment undertaken by the service provider. Mode 4 is presence of natural persons covering foreign labour services in Abu Dhabi.

Innovative services crossing borders are due to agglomeration and location as in sovereign wealth funds deploying capital in acquisitions abroad. According to China, digesting transferred knowledge is more than ownership. But by following the East Asian "flying geese" pattern of economic development[2] led by Japan, we can say that "regionness" matters for direct foreign investment and multinational corporations.

Agglomeration beyond clustering is evident in industrial clusters and free zones (Chapter 2) as mixed developments rather than an old

---

[2]Like birds migrating to warmer places in winter in a triangular flight pattern, Japan led the pack of high-performing Asian economies. As Japan climbed up its industrial ladder, it relocated labour-intensive industries to South Korea and Taiwan in turn passing some to Southeast Asia which continues to supply Japan with raw materials, production bases and markets in a very unique geographical and cultural fashion.

brick-and-mortar economy based on goods. From production-based to knowledge-based with innovation (Fig. 1.1), agglomeration is the synergy of a critical aggregative mass arising from lumpiness of economies of scale or network externality.

Agglomeration includes "new economic geography"[3] in a related, but distinct concept of external scale effects that arises from public infrastructure. Innovation is a social system comprising interrelated individuals, informal groups, organisations, and/or subsystems. It can be in linear sequences of time-order of phases or by serendipity.[4] Even culture and mindset change are critical aspects in managing innovation in intangible knowledge-based services.

A few other economic laws, including Moore's law[5] apply to information communication technology with globalisation and connectivity (Emirates Centre for Strategic Studies and Research, 2008c; Lupia *et al.*, 2007) to enhance productivity or reduce inflation. A "tradability revolution"[6] enables service production and distribution

---

[3]Economic geography is the study of the location, distribution and spatial organisation of economic activities across the world, spawning growth triangles as in Southeast Asia and cross-border production networks as division of labour and specialisation including hyper-competition as non-price quality, standards, timeliness, safety, or security.

[4]*Warfarin* drug which inhibits the synthesis of clotting factors and prevents blood clot formation happened by serendipity (Everett, 1995, p 50).

[5]In Moore's Law, the processing power of silicon chip doubles every 18 months, so affordable communication network and internet applications rise. Carlson's curve may be the genetic equivalent of Moore's law. Productivity in DNA sequencing and synthesis techniques enables bacteria to produce human proteins which in turn produce new pharmaceuticals and drugs. Grossman's paradox sees there will always be a market for information by dismissing the self-contradictory assumption of perfect information under perfect competition. People can never know it all, or at least, they can never know that they know it all. Endless information is produced. Reed's law states that the utility scale of large networks is exponential with the size of network externality or third-party transactions.

[6]What used to be nontradable from houses to infrastructure built in one location, not physically movable across borders are as easily bought and sold by liberalised ownership laws or traded as financial products and derivatives with mortgages and securitisation intermediated by banks.

globally via outsourcing (Taplin, ed, 2008),[7] offshoring,[8] software clusters,[9] internet economies,[10] and virtual states.[11]

In contrast to generally favourable trends and developments, the parallel for financial services in particular is cautioned. With Abu Dhabi, Dubai and Bahrain aiming to be global financial centres, the literature on misadventures leading to the global financial crisis is clear (Barbera, 2009; Hyman, 1986; Kindleberger, 1977, 1978; Fischer, 2005; Brunnermeier, 2009, 2001; Gorton, 2008, 2010; Kashyap *et al.*, 2010).

3.2. Finance, Banking, Insurance, and Islamic Finance

Saadiyat Island did not take-off as a financial free zone, probably an idea ahead of its time. A financial district in Sowwah island is a part of

---

[7]Outsourcing to other service providers within the national boundaries allows an entity to focus on its core competitive competencies.

[8]Off-shoring is outsourcing noncore activities to firms abroad. It means job and income loss, but compensated by higher productivity gains at the core or the firms owning or establishing the foreign affiliates as "captive off-shoring" through direct foreign investment.

[9]Innovations and networks in knowledge-intensive clusters are further hybridised as offshoring-based as in Bangalore (Akifumi *et al.*, eds, 2010, pp. 204–227).

[10]The internet economy is built on four layers; (a) internet infrastructure as internet backbone of service providers, networking hardware and software companies, personal computer and server manufacturers, security vendors and fiber optic makers; (b) internet applications including internet consultants, internet commerce applications, multimedia applications, web development software, search engine software, online training, web-enabled databases; (c) internet intermediary comprising market makers in vertical industries, online travel agents, online brokerages, content aggregators, portals/content providers, internet advertisement brokers, and online advertising; and (d) internet commerce as e-tailers, manufacturers online, fee/subscription-based companies, airlines online tickets, online entertainment and professional services. Security concern is a trade-off (Abdulla, 2009).

[11]A virtual state like Singapore (Low, 2002, 2000) with limited land, but highly wired by information communication technology has globalisation morphed with regionalisation through ideas, technology, finance, and people moving with politics and social relations. It increasingly relocates part of its production abroad to reshape both productive and international relationships. Electronic highways and wireless access extend spatial distances.

Plan Abu Dhabi 2030. Financial services as a whole contributed 5.8% to Abu Dhabi's GDP in 2009 (Table 2.1). While it lags behind real estate and business (by 8.4%), it could catch-up in property related financial products and upgraded productivity via e-banking. Even remittances are expedited by e-transfers is traditional trust-based *hawala*[12] going high-technology.

Attracting professional and high skilled Emiratis into financial services, especially in Islamic banking and *takaful* Sharia-compliant insurance needs some cultural and work reorientation. Competitive market forces are best to ensure qualified rather than a token emiratisation quota of 5% for banks. The financial sector is inherently cosmopolitan, especially by dominant foreign clientele.

The Abu Dhabi banking sector has many small-sized banks, unlike Saudi Arabia or Kuwait which have less than 10 large, well-capitalised banks. They need to grow in size for economies of scale to finance big-ticket deals. At the other end of the spectrum, large local banks are government-owned, the biggest is the National Bank of Abu Dhabi by assets as among the more mature, highly profitable, steadfast banks.[13]

The Abu Dhabi Commercial Bank is 65% owned by the Abu Dhabi Investment Authority. It is involved in some privatisation projects of the Abu Dhabi Water and Electricity Authority and Dolphin project. It expanded its capital base in a rights issue in 2005[14] and

---

[12] *Hawala* as a nonbank domain is not regulated as financial firms, but culturally significant, especially for low-skilled South Asians. The UAE has obligations to the International Monetary Fund's Anti-Money Laundering and Combating the Financing of Terrorism.

[13] The National Petroleum Construction Company got Dh404 million to build a vessel for offshore oil operations in loans from the Abu Dhabi National Leasing Company of the National Bank of Abu Dhabi; *The National*, April 10, 2011.

[14] Prior to the global financial crisis, Abu Dhabi Commercial Bank reported a 2005 half-year profitability of 178%, net interest margin increase of 50% and fee income by 4.5 times due to fees from initial public offers, only 15% without such fees. Throughout the years up to the global financial crisis, Abu Dhabi banks were reporting such triple-digit growth rates; unsurprising if these are simple growth rates rather than the compound annual rates of growth.

provisioned for up to 25% for foreign ownership. Another state-owned is First Gulf Bank that shares the same chairman as UAE Offsets Group. State-owned Hilal Bank, founded in 2009, is the newest, despite UAE banks claiming an overbanked sector of 47 banks.

The retail banking sector remains as the staple growth area, without many saving and investment options other than speculation in bubbly real estate and stock exchanges. Passively relying on basic services versus proactively enhancing output and sales is neither strategic nor sustainable. Fees for loans in initial public offers, profits from takeovers, acquisitions or mergers are not organic growth. Abu Dhabi banks violated Central Bank's guideline on loan ceilings for initial public offers in 2005 and 2006.[15]

A solid organic path is derived from project financing that includes mobilising pension funds, specialising in export credit and insurance, industrial or start-up loans to finesse Vision 2030 projects. The Abu Dhabi Islamic Bank which also owns *Takaful* Insurance strikes a right chord in starting export financing as others follow suit in other packages for small and medium-sized firms (Chapter 4). Abu Dhabi banks cannot take for granted the high margins in a low-interest rate environment by the fixed dirham-dollar peg.[16]

Despite clear banking laws and directives, poor enforcement and *wasta* or relation-based lending, resulted in faulty non-performing loans. Corporate governance as accountability and transparency is an omission in letter and spirit. While many banks have replaced core

---

[15]After one 2005 initial public offer, the UAE Central Bank confiscated illegal bank profits from lending beyond the 1:5 permitted ratio: 20% bank loan and 80% investor fund. For sensitivity reason, it did not name violating banks. It is a classic moral hazard situation as a lender-of-last-resort with bailouts by a central bank, not a monetary moral-guardian-of-first-resort.

[16]The UAE Central Bank has repeatedly signalled no change to the fixed exchange rate regime or de-peg from the dollar. It means no independent monetary policy, except the UAE mimicking US interest rates despite their diametrically opposite economic conditions, respectively, boom with inflation and recession. Its *ad hoc* panel of four international experts remains in dispute since 2010, with no sign of resumption of review, not at least without some GCC-wide signal or political will, be it paralysis by analysis or lack of wherewithal to manage any new exchange rate policy.

systems in the early 2000s, it is doubtful that outdated legacy systems may have been capable of capturing the granular level of data and statistics required for trend analysis.

The infrastructure for e-banking enabled high utilisation rates of automated-teller-machines (ATMs), transactions over mobile telephones, and internet banking. Streamlined modern banking practices including an image cheque-clearing system are in place, but banks still lack transparency in hidden bank service fees. The expatriate majority often make the wrong assumption that banking practices in the UAE are the same as those at home.

Abu Dhabi banks were generally unscathed in the global financial crisis, except for some.[17] Some countries have an insurance credit shield or insurance depository system for depositor confidence to avert bank from running into crises. The Department of Finance injected liquidity into banks with a blanket of guarantee for all, in addition to a Dh120 billion emergency fund facilitated by the UAE Central Bank and Ministry of Finance[18] as standard operating procedure.

Post-crisis, bank consolidations are unlikely,[19] given the local environment and culture which eschew bankruptcy. The UAE Central Bank has spruced up commercial bank lending, deemed the most

---

[17] Abu Dhabi Commercial Bank reported its exposure to Dubai World's announcing on November 25, 2009 to delay its loan repayments and the debacle between Saudi conglomerates Saad Group and Ahmad Hamad Al Gosaibi and Brothers; *The National*, January 29, 2010. Dubai World's unravelling ultimately led to massive restructuring (not equivalent to bankruptcy) of Dubai Inc, all over exposed to a bubbly real estate.

[18] Dh16 billion was injected into five state-owned Abu Dhabi-based banks, Abu Dhabi Commercial Bank, Abu Dhabi Islamic Bank, First Gulf Bank, National Bank of Abu Dhabi, and Union National Bank. UAE banks not suffering from deposit withdrawal did not use the emergency liquidity facility. After tightening lending and more provisions for nonperforming loans, they gradually restored their generally high capital adequacy levels averaging 18–19%; *Khaleej Times*, February 5 and December 21, 2009.

[19] Talks started in May 2010, but failed as the merger of Al Khaliji Commercial Bank and International Bank of Qatar is ended with no agreement on the final terms. It was to help to stabilise a fractured banking sector, with 1.4 million residents served by 18 Qatari banks. Neither is there news of a long-rumoured merger of Islamic banking units; *The National*, June 8, 2011.

radical shake-up of the banking industry in years. As part of the global regulatory trend, it put retail bank caps to 20 times the monthly salary and loan-repayment period to a maximum of 48 months in April 2011.

A month later, new mortgage rules to avert more speculative bubbles impose different loan limits for first-time buyers for owner-occupied housing and investors for investment. The Central Bank relented for existing loans to be grandfathered into the new rules, applied only to new loans after May 1, 2011.[20] A retail banking committee was formed to consult the industry more regularly for future regulation. Despite anecdotally high household indebtedness with easy credit cards and loans, more lending to expatriates was allowed versus a previous limit of Dh250,000 that was set in 1993.

As generally true across-the-board, the Central Bank lacks effective and efficient enforcement of rules. Without a credit bureau, banks have insufficient information of total loans and repayments, past history and behavior in payment of customers. The jury is still out for a credit rating bureau and corporate rating bureau in Abu Dhabi. A joint venture in credit rating was aborted in 2005 by the then Department of Economy which left Abu Dhabi with the UAE Central Bank's inadequate credit rating services or Dubai's Emcredit by 2010.

Central Bank regulations disallowed banks to make cold-calls to the public in order to market new offers. Telemarketing calls remain permissible, but still irritating for existing customers. A better and more intelligent revenue stream is targeted cross-selling based on customers' needs, not dumping new products without analysing segmented markets.

This needs diligent collation of statistics and a suite of analytic tools on spending and saving patterns to predict who needs a specific product from a loan to topping-up pre-paid cards. Professionalism and behavioural science more than plain marketing to score sales means a return to customer service standards as banks compete for sustainable relationships for a peripatetic clientele.

Banking was easy, seemingly a lost art in a decade-long property bubble. The global financial crisis perversely was a blessing in disguise

---

[20]The First Gulf Bank's existing loan book was reported as Dh35 billion or $9.52 billion; *The National*, May 18 and 29, 2011.

leading to better banking services. The seismic wake-up call portends an upgraded sophistry in financial output and products with international standards, benchmarks and best practices. Yet, many banks are still exposed to real estate by owning and leasing out commercial buildings as revenue streams.

The Bank of International Settlements in 2011 revised new Basel III rules on capital adequacy. It effectively raised the total common equity requirement from 2% to 7%, comprising both pillars of minimum common equity requirement and capital conservation buffer. It introduced a third as countercyclical buffer according to national circumstances.

Transition to Basel III would first require Abu Dhabi to include the Basel III into its existing laws followed by its implementation in 2018 to avert "casino mad money"-like situation. It is the oldest delusion since the Dutch tulip mania (Dash, 1999, 2000) as a classic Ponzi or pyramid scheme,[21] all on a slippery slope. Most Abu Dhabi banks with a capital adequacy ratio above 8% have no problem with Basel II or Base III. A credit crunch with bank liquidity persists, not helping any recovery since the global financial crisis.

As the UAE Central Bank introduces macro-prudential regulation for stability of the financial system, it needs to go beyond Basel III capital adequacy ratio which is time consuming. More focus is on quality risk management capabilities and a stringent evaluation process. GCC banks could heed stress tests, transparency, market discipline as corporate governance and encouraging competition for state-owned banks.

Risk management following greater uncertainty with a global fragile recovery means radical reengineering. Financial innovations[22] have extended willy-nilly into all forms of insurance, mortgages,

---

[21]Tulipmania was in 1624, Ponzi after Charles Ponzi in 1919 is similar to a pyramid scheme. Both are based on using new investors' funds to pay earlier backers. One difference is a Ponzi scheme gathers funds from new investors then distributes them. A pyramid plan allows each investor to directly benefit depending on number of new investors recruited and whoever is on top does not have access to all the money in the system. The scam in all eventually is not enough money to go around, so schemes unravel.

[22] *The Economist.* http://www.economist.com/debate/days/view/471, February 23, 2010.

securitisation, derivatives, arbitrage and hedging, hedge funds, shorting,[23] and commodity trading.

Not all financial innovations are bad. Advances in mathematical financial theory and behavioural finance are boon and bane for risk management. There is a scarcity of qualified professionals to facilitate the transition to a higher corporate governance and orientation to risk.[24] Well-designed, structured laws and regulations are needed for an efficient array of complementary and supplementary market tools.

In Islamic banking, the UAE champions are led by the Dubai Islamic Bank,[25] Abu Dhabi Islamic Bank, Emirates Islamic Bank and Sharjah Islamic Bank.[26] Islamic financial services have vibrant growth and potential, especially in the Middle East by population and wealth. The region as a whole lacks clear regulatory procedures to proactively access untapped funds.

The legal and conceptual definition of Islamic banks needs more clarity. Separate legal entities established within conventional banking standard operating procedures, principles and schemes create uncertain relationship among banks and regulators. Accounting principles involving revenue realisation, disclosure of accounting bases and valuation, profit and loss of shares of depositors are fuzzy without clear supervision.

---

[23]Short selling is selling of a security which the seller does not own, or any sale that is completed by the delivery of a security borrowed by the seller. It assumes that the short sellers are able to buy the stock at a price lower than the price at which they sold short. It is the opposite of going long, as short sellers make money if the stock goes down in price. It is an advanced trading strategy with unique risks and pitfalls.

[24]The UAE has only six qualified financial risk managers certified by the US Global Association of Risk Professionals as a network of over 150,000 members in 195 countries in October 2010: http://www.garp.org.

[25]Dubai Islamic Bank, reported as the largest in the UAE launched Emirates Real Estate Investment Trust in 2010, but its net profit in 2010 plummeted 33% year-on-year; *Gulf News*, March 12, 2011.

[26]Blominvest bank SAL in 2009 reported total assets of Islamic banking at $250 billion to reach $1 trillion by 2016. Of this, the GCC countries account for nearly 56% of the total Islamic banking assets, a majority of which in turn are accounted by the top-three Islamic banks alone, namely, Al Rajhi Bank, Kuwait Finance House and Dubai Islamic Bank.

There is no one Islamic banking model with varying interpretations of Shariah laws. An Islamic Financial Board like that in Malaysia in 2002 could enhance and coordinate developmental initiatives, speed up operations, and risk management. Initiating processes to customise country-specific models for new market segments, new products, capital market development as in bonds or *sukuk* would inject professionalism and integrity.

The ability to respond more efficiently to increasingly sophisticated client demands and compete more effectively with conventional banking requires regulatory gaps to be filled by a central Shariah board with supervisory guidelines. Getting Shariah scholars, jurists, and bankers to come together is by no mean a feat, aggravated by a sheer shortage of such professionals in the first place.

As asset-based with tangible collateral, Islamic banking is neither speculative nor usury to counter conventional greed and irrational exuberance. Developing products in the fullness of time would meet rising demand in the mortgage market. Property laws in Abu Dhabi and Dubai need more work on credible strata title deeds.

Equally promising is *takaful* Shariah-compliant insurance. The insurance sector has taken off with national health insurance for all in Abu Dhabi since 2005. To attract more Emiratis into the insurance industry, Dubai SME as an agency of Dubai's Department of Economic Development, mandated to develop small and medium-sized enterprises sector, has a memorandum of understanding with Noor *Takaful*.[27] Abu Dhabi's Department of Economic Development is forming two agencies for export and investment, which are likely to partner banks and insurance firms.

New products like commercial banks in insurance or "bankassurance" by the Citibank, American International Group, Allianz, ING and Fortis, or "assurebanking" by insurance companies selling banking products as pure investment have evolved in Asia and other emerging markets. Making a virtue of large expatriate community to

---

[27] It offers flexible business start-up options in franchises to UAE nationals to sell Noor Takaful branded products, with awareness programmes and understanding of a franchise model; *The National*, June 8, 2011.

offer new saving and investment products would retain some remittances or direct some into start-ups with oft-repeated room for specialised industrial finance.

Given Abu Dhabi's extensive investment in infrastructure and other commercial projects in the region extending to India and Pakistan, its strategy can be an economic and financial string of pearls for more value-added.[28] The large pool of Muslims and even non-Muslims for Islamic banking as an economic string of pearls suffices for now. It will be generalised across-the-board for Abu Dhabi's model for economic development with asset acquisitions abroad later (Chapter 5).

Ambitions have to be realistic to global contexts. For an upgrade from the Morgan Stanley Capital International (MSCI)[29] frontier to emerging market, the UAE stock markets need more foreign ownership than 3.3% in listed firms and a new settlement system as delivery-versus payment for same day payment and delivery. An upgrade means better regulated and more liquid bourses to attract fresh funds.

Abu Dhabi alone cannot make any meaningful financial sector reform without the Ministry of Economy, Central Bank and Dubai as a law unto itself. Capital is mobile and fungible. A case in point is how stock markets are connected with globalised ownership and e-transactions (see Fig. 3.1).

Abu Dhabi Securities Exchange is in alliance with New York Stock Exchange Euronext, itself partly owned by Qatar Stock Exchange which also has a stake in London Stock Exchange, in turn linked to Dubai's stock exchange. Borse Dubai owns both the Dubai Financial Market and Nasdaq Dubai, linked to New York Stock Exchange Euronext.

---

[28] The analogy is like China's string of pearls in its acquisitions of energy and other natural resources from Africa, Latin America to the Middle East Iran and its investment in infrastructure in South Asia. It is seen by its South Asian neighbours, especially Pakistan as a geopolitical and security encirclement. Unlike China as a superpower, Abu Dhabi's economic string of pearls has no real threats, but opportunities for all.

[29] The MSCI Global Equity Indices cover over 400 exchanged traded funds in over 70 countries in the developed, emerging and frontier markets. Morocco and Egypt are the only Middle East markets as emerging; UAE's upgrade is delayed again from mid- to end-2011; *The National*, June 21 and 23, 2011.

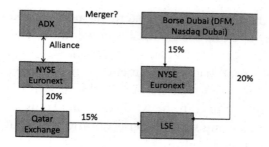

Figure 3.1 UAE stock exchanges.

Drawn: Drawn by author.

Both the federal Emirates Securities and Commodities Authority and Abu Dhabi Securities Exchange regulate stock markets in Abu Dhabi.

The full-scale integration of Dubai Financial Market and Nasdaq Dubai creates an equity trading platform. Since the global financial crisis, size, and competitiveness mean more than the sum of individual parts.[30] The Abu Dhabi Securities Exchange apparent support of a possible merger with Dubai's exchange for the same multiplier effects has not gone further. The Gulf stock exchanges have generally bypassed consolidation as a trend started in the West as beneficial for investors, issuers, and regulators.

The Abu Dhabi Securities Exchange has reclassified its listed company sectors in line with industry-preferred sector definitions, designed a certification programme to show its commitment to education and training and a new code for capital adequacy norms. This was done to establish a separate National Central Securities Depository and Registry in order to pursue cross-listings with other GCC exchanges and cross-border settlements.

---

[30] Of the two merged entities, Dubai Financial Market is 80% owned by Borse Dubai and the rest of 20% listed on the Dubai Financial Market, while Nasdaq Dubai 100% owned by Dubai Financial Market. The new holding company is 100%-owned by Borse Dubai which also owns 21% of the London Stock Exchange and 19.9% of Nasdaq OMX Group. The merger is rationalised as Nasdaq Dubai's low trading volumes since its inception is able to access Dubai Financial Market's asset classes with cross-exchange listing following rules, regulations and governance set by Nasdaq Dubai; *Gulf News*, May 10 and 20, 2010.

The UAE has an unwieldy system of multiple regulators which could become a competitive disadvantage in a costly regulatory mousetrap. A mechanism to control stock market transactions could be similar to a central bank department to supervise banks. How the relevant regulators work together, preferably at arm's length without conflict of interests[31] need to be worked upon. Transparent corporate governance in a growing stakeholder economy needs public education as part of a shareholder culture.

The UAE is the most responsive in implementing GCC integration mechanisms. The federal Emirates Securities and Commodities Authority has ratified a decision to treat GCC nationals and GCC brokerages as locals in the UAE stock markets. This could help in creating the GCC common market and greater liquidity on stock exchanges. The UAE gesture is yet to be reciprocated by other GCC states, that is, for Emiratis to enjoy the same local privileges as GCC citizens elsewhere.

A more pressing and concerted effort is for Abu Dhabi to link the large real estate sector to the financial and equity markets more sustainably rather than in speculative bubbles. Banks have to be more developmental than operating in a passively myopic sector, latched to oil wealth, liquidity and profits from initial public offers. Developing new competitive financial products needs financial sophistication. Habits have to be aligned from banks to end-users, not just the gadgetry of e-banking services.

As a whole, the finance, banking, and insurance sector is relatively protected. Foreign bank branches as 100%-owned pay a 20% income tax, exempted for national banks. The sector is obligated to the WTO as telecommunication services to open up for competition, if not foreign ownership. Corporate governance means international standards, benchmarks, best practices in accounting and auditing.[32]

---

[31] Board members in regulatory exchanges as owners or chairmen of listed firm have a conflict of interest.

[32] Dubai Financial Services Authority regulates Dubai International Financial Centre, using audit standards laid down by the UK Association of Certified Chartered Accountants to frame its guidelines. It is dubbed by the UAE Central Bank as the "closest thing there is to the Vatican in concept".

3.3. Financial Sector Development and Capital Deepening

Long-term finance for long-term Vision 2030 projects needs matching maturities of corporate and sovereign bond markets, specialised funds and venture capital to deepen capital markets beside private equity. Emiratis have wealth. All need knowledge for start-up funds to actualise projects. Less focus on speculative real estate and consumer financing and more focus to industrial financing is a remiss by commercial banks.

Financial and capital market deepening involves financial sophistication. Proceed with knowledge, due-diligence care is cautioned, but made difficult as the process of making laws and regulations is long, tedious without enforcement as a strong suit.

To attract private equity funds, they need exit options, generally accompanied by a primary offer or public listing by a firm of its shares to the new investors. It is not smooth in development as the *raison d'etre* and logic of public flotation needs a rethink more than for wealth distribution. Emiratis are yet to cultivate a stakeholder culture. More relevantly, it is a paradigm shift in regulatory infrastructure for equity and capital market deepening.

With or without the global financial crisis, more self-financing by autonomous entities seek private equity and venture capital funds. These need at least two exit routes to divest and move to new investment opportunities, unlike long-term Abu Dhabi Inc stakeholders with patient capital. These options are raised and discussed by private equity funds at the initial consideration of an opportunity. They are evaluated in-house in a pre-acquisition, due diligence and approval process.

The majority of exits are through trade sales as a disposal of the entire share capital to a third party purchaser, mostly in the same industry. They bring a higher valuation to the company that is being sold more than a full stock market quotation. A prospective purchaser needs the valuation to supplement his/her own business.

Repurchase of private equity fund shares in a company by another may include the original firm's management team. Secondary buy-out, re-capitalisation or re-financing means the firm acquired by an existing management team is backed by equity finance from new private equity providers. New debt/mezzanine finance substitutes are funds from the new lenders at a later-stage sale and purchase transaction.

More sophisticated options like securitisation enable investors to consider returns on investment without a typical exit transaction like secondary trading of participation in private equity limited partnership funds. It allows investors to realise cash from otherwise illiquid investment and not wait for distribution from realisation of individual portfolios. Involuntary exit is where a company goes into receivership or liquidation.

Investors look to exit between 3–7 years from acquisition date. Straightforward expectations have exit valued as critical, as soon as commercial objectives allow for it. In most scenarios, a private equity fund juggles between achieving an early exit or allowing a company to mature and increase value over time. Generally, it prefers certainty of early exit to slightly higher valuation over a longer period.

Successful exits depend on rectifying concerns raised in due diligence and ensure parameters are agreed to create a viable framework for exits. During the investment period, private equity funds as part of an acquisition, means a need to learn and understand what makes a company valuable, and what to do to increase long-term value with an eye always on exit.

Private equity funds in association with the management will seek to monitor due diligence, improve fiduciary responsibility and establish management share options schemes for incentives for management. It follows stringent accounting policies, industry-specific corporate governance in relationships with key customers and suppliers and resolve all issues which otherwise be a drag on companies.

Post-acquisition, all parties are focused on the goal of successful exit. Private equity funds know successful exit needs full management support and participation. To secure certainty, exit aspirations are aired from the outset of investment, documented in definitive agreements with various provisions to facilitate exit terms, protect position and exit as soon as commercially practicable.

Private equity funds may incorporate a right to require a company to initiate exit after an agreed-upon time period. They routinely demand and get drag-along rights enabling them to require sale of an entire capital even if shareholders disagree, termed as dragged to sell. The option to deliver an entire share capital versus a minority or majority stake is critical to sourcing a potential third-party purchaser and achieving greater value.

Definitive agreements may include tag-along or bring-along rights. They enable private equity funds to require all or part of shares to be sold if any other shareholder intends to sell, otherwise no such sales are permissible. Agreements may contain liquidation and sale preferences clauses under which private equity funds entitled to a priority return from proceeds of liquidation or sale of company.

Without such knowledge, the initial public offer window remains a myth for most Gulf entrepreneurs. Market research, data, sophisticated valuation models, and independent equity analysts are nonexistent. Prospectus of private sector initial public offers gives flimsy disclosures to invite class-action lawsuits. This is unlikely only because they are confined to wealth distribution for Emiratis. Existing regulations oblige shares to be allocated on a pro-rata basis; nationals receive approximately 0.2% of the offer tabled.

The Ministry of Economy mandates that initial public offer shares must be sold at a discount at par value of Dh1. It is a flawed one-price assumption. Shares priced at par leads investors to buy any stock without being sufficiently discerning about the companies that they are buying into. Coupled with excess demand, frenzy selling follows to reap capital gains. That is not toward a long-term equity culture.

The regulations have actually hurt the small investors, which they should have prevented. They pay a 0.5% bank fee for underwriting services on overleveraged bank loans.[33] Ironically, oversubscribed subscriptions are deemed by the market as successful high demand. Artificial oversubscription priced at Dh1 and penalising the resultant bank commissions is treating symptoms of misplaced market correc-

---

[33] The cost of the large unutilised credit for the Aldar initial public offer in 2004 was estimated at $518 million with 80% overleveraged. Thus, the Aldar stock price had to quadruple before investors get their money back; not impossible with the frenzied boom then, but most positions are so small that they may be hardly worth selling.

tion, not curing portfolio speculative capital.[34] Episodes are summarily dismissed, not mitigated.

More serious thought and changes are needed for family-owned business to go public. The benefits include tapping liquidity and buoyancy in the market, attract long-term direct foreign investment with the transfers of technology and management skills and markets for more sustainable income and jobs.

A wariness to foreign partnership remains. Families fear losing control by diluting ownership in listing. The mandated 55% divestment rule remained until the Ministry of Economy struck a mid-way of 30%. But the Dubai International Financial Exchange mandates only 25%.

A second tier stock market in addition to the Abu Dhabi main board can help small and medium-sized enterprises, start-ups and small family-owned firms. It means less onerous listing criteria for initial public offers like the Stock Exchange of Singapore Deal and Quotation. Another suggestion is for Abu Dhabi real estate investment trusts.[35] The Dubai International Financial Exchange already lists them since 2006.

A positive development is Abu Dhabi issuing its first $3 billion five-year and 10-year government bonds as part of its $10 billion programme in April 2009. Standard & Poor's, Fitch Ratings and

---

[34] The 600 million initial public offer shares of the Abu Dhabi National Energy Company, Taqa in 2005 was a classic privatisation power symbol to deepen capital markets, give nationals a stake in the industrial renaissance and downstream energy ventures and benchmark to create equity culture; in short, a potential successful template for corporate governance. Instead, it triggered speculative bubbles and shut out nationals as Asian expatriates fraudulently used unsuspecting nationals' names to apply for shares.

[35] A real estate investment trust is defined as a security which sells like a stock on major exchanges and invests in real estate directly either through properties or mortgages. Its gets around the lack of mortgage transfer through securitisation. The most common is equity real estate investment trust. It invests in, and owns properties to be responsible for the equity or value of these real estate assets with revenue principally from rent. A mortgage real estate investment trust deals in investment and ownership of property mortgages, loan money for mortgages to owners of real estate, or invests in (purchases) existing mortgages or mortgage backed securities. Revenue is primarily from interest on mortgage loans. A hybrid combines both investment strategies to invest in properties and mortgages.

Moody's Investors Services had assigned their third-highest rating available as "AA" or "Aa2" to reflect Abu Dhabi's financial strength.

It was a test of how the global financial crisis affected its economic development and Vision 2030.[36] More important than proving credit worthiness is the sovereign bond as part of the book-building process. It sets a yield curve as the basis for other corporate bonds by banks or telecommunication firms as long-term capital market deepening.[37]

3.4. Tourism, Wholesale and Retail Trade

Abu Dhabi is a recent entrant in the field of tourism like the Middle East which is generally a laggard in global tourism (Sharpley, 2002) except Dubai and Saudi Arabia for *haj* and *umrah*. Dubai as an urban exciting "happening" place is mature and sophisticated, going up the value chain to great heights and scale, literally in buildings. Developing tourism[38] is an emirate-level preoccupation in distinctive models and strategies.

Abu Dhabi wants to balance tradition and values, not erosion as a fast-paced urban tourism hub. Its tourism brand and tourism master plan reflect a comfort level in its philosophy and direction. Hotels and restaurants contributed 1.2% to Abu Dhabi's GDP in 2009 (Table 2.2) with 5.5% by wholesale, retail trade, both adding to 6.7%.[39]

---

[36] *Gulf News*, March 31, 2009.

[37] Beside bonds of state-owned banks, in 2011, Aabar Investments is to issue €750 million in bonds convertible into shares in Daimler, to cut its 9.1% stake in 2009 to 8%, as the bonds represent 1.1% of all outstanding Daimler shares; *The National*, May 25, 2011.

[38] A 10% tourism levy is collected by hotels and hotel serviced apartments on behalf of the government. Only restaurants for tourists are allowed to impose a 15% service charge which they can keep in lieu of tips. An airport tax of Dh30 per passenger applies.

[39] The Statistics Centre Abu Dhabi has ways to go before input–output tables for interindustry linkages and a tourism satellite account. It is a framework for policy-makers and entrepreneurs as a set of concepts, definitions, classifications and tables to articulate a set of economic (monetary) flows traced from the consumption unit (inbound and outbound visitors) to the productive unit (industries producing and/ or importing goods and services for visitors) with multiplier analysis.

Table 3.1.   Projected visitors and tourists in Abu Dhabi by airport arrivals.

Visitors	2006	2007	2008	2009	2010	2011	2012
Total '000	1,609	1,728	2,053	2,500	2,950	3,282	3,404
Residents %	13	17	19	19	20	21	21
Tourists %	84	83	81	81	80	79	79

Source: The Abu Dhabi Economic Vision 2030, http://www.abudhabi.ae.

The Abu Dhabi Travel and Tourism Agencies Committee established in 2000 is supported by the Civil Aviation Department. It is recognised by the Abu Dhabi Chamber of Commerce and Industry and Abu Dhabi Municipality.

The Abu Dhabi Tourism Authority formed in 2005 regulates tourism activities. It has opened many international offices in the UK, Germany, and France and planning more in Asia. Vision 2030 has Abu Dhabi to be a world-class destination with the promotion and marketing of its brand. A forecast of 3 million visitors and tourists by 2012 (Table 3.1) is based on compound annual growth rates of 13.3%, 18.2%, and 12.2%, respectively for total, resident visitors and tourists.

A law in 2005 established the Abu Dhabi National Exhibition Company (Ma'arid) as a subsidiary of the Abu Dhabi Tourism Authority. It has Dh10 billion in capital for 50 years (can be shortened or renewed) to promote local, regional, and international exhibitions.[40] Its first phase was completed in 2006 which added to half of its target of 57,000 square meters in gross exhibition costing Dh500 million.

Another subsidiary of the Abu Dhabi Tourism Authority is the Tourism Development and Investment Company since 2006 as a master developer of major tourism destinations.[41] Its projects include Saadiyat Island to house the world's largest single concentration of

---

[40] The new law abrogated the General Exhibition Corporation formed under Law No. 3 of 1998 and all its employees, assets, rights, and obligations transferred over to Ma'arid.

[41] The Tourism Development and Investment Company has investment grade ratings of Aa2, AA, and AA by three top credit rating agencies, Moody's, Standard & Poor and Fitch, respectively, enabling it to launch a $3 billion Global Medium Term Note (GMTN) programme for its investment arm.

premier cultural institutions, including Zayed National Museum, Louvre Abu Dhabi, Guggenheim Abu Dhabi, Performing Arts Centre and Maritime Museum. A group of natural islands off the long coast of Abu Dhabi's Al Gharbia, including Sir Bani Yas Island and Desert Islands are nature-based destinations as naturally beautiful.

With Eithad Airlines[42] launched as Abu Dhabi's national carrier, a differentiated strategy, image, and brand as an alternative embraces eco-tourism, safety and security in friendly Islamic culture and values. Abu Dhabi aims for leisure-cum-business, family-based and high-end niche markets, not mass tourism.

Demographically, the international pool of babyboomers (those born between 1946 and 1964) is a potential market segment. Some retire with finance and time to have summer homes in the region. Abu Dhabi has to look East beyond traditional Europe. Tourists from China[43] more than Japan are the Asian next wave. One focus is Muslim and non-Muslim in the Far East.

The lack of Abu Dhabi recreation facilities is solved by tourism activities and events, both for locals and visitors. It integrates tourism with the local culture and values. Infrastructure development has over-arching benefits, in education, health, religion, culture, environment, marine, sea sports, and recreational types of tourism. Abu Dhabi, Al Ain, and Dubai in the first instance, is one package of UAE-based recreation.

3.5. Transport, Telecommunication and Logistics

Transport, telecommunication, and logistics as a whole is at the heart of Vision 2030's knowledge-based economy from Eithad Airlines, Sky City, and Media City to e-business and e-commerce expedited by the telecommunication revolution. Abu Dhabi's metro (Abu Dhabi,

---

[42] Abu Dhabi divested in 2005 in the Bahrain loss-making Gulf Air as Qatar did in 2002, to start Etihad Airlines. Its routes complement and supplement Dubai's Emirates Airlines without co-sharing in general.
[43] China may grant the Approved Destination Status to the UAE, already given to Egypt and Jordan.

2009, http//www.abudhabi.ae) is in the making with Etihad Railway for the UAE to be linked to the GCC railway network eventually. In 2009, it contributed 7.1% to its GDP, which is the second-largest in the services sector (Table 2.1).

More than traditional roads and highways, ports are servicing the flow of goods and people. Suffice to note is intellectual property rights at the federal level, same as *etisalat* and *du* as federal-owned are forging ahead to support all emirates. A convergence in the value chain for information communication technology covers content, service, infrastructure, and terminal at the end-user's premises.

As aviation landing rights affect national security, they are negotiated bilaterally by governments rather under GATS. An open sky policy is neither easy nor simple with eight degrees of freedom to be negotiated (Doganis, 2001).[44]

The trio of Emirates, Etihad, and Qatar Airlines considered as *bête noir* by other legacy carriers compete strongly[45] in long-neglected routes to developing economies and as alternatives to other local airlines. They do enjoy lower operating costs as labour and access to finance by export credit-backed deals which are barred for Europe airlines.

The emerging triple-play of transport-telecommunication-tourism implies that all data, voice, and video services will finally converge in

---

[44]They are rights to fly over another country without landing; make a landing for technical reasons (refuelling) in another country without picking up/setting down revenue traffic; carry revenue traffic from own country (A) to country (B) of treaty partner; right to carry traffic from country B back to your own country A; airline from country A to carry revenue traffic between country B and other countries such as C or D on services starting or ending in its home country A (this freedom cannot be used unless countries C or D also agree); use by an airline of country A of two sets of 3rd and 4th freedom rights to carry traffic between two other countries but using its base at (A) as a transit point; airline to carry revenue traffic between points in two countries on services which lie entirely outside its own home country; and cabotage rights for an airline to pick up and set down passenger or freight between two domestic points in another country on a service originating in its own home country.

[45]Both UAE airlines are locked a five-year battle to get more landing rights in Canada: *International Herald Tribune*, October 12, 2010 and December 2, 2011; *Gulf News*, January 15, 2011 and March 9, 2011; *Khaleej Times*, December 28, 2010 and January 23, 2011; and *The National*, January 12, 2011 and May 24, 2011.

an intellectual property-based next-generation-network. A quadruple-play will stress on the involvement of mobility plus wireless connectivity at the next level. In mobile technology, the UAE has second- and third generation and general packet-switched radio services.[46] It lacks enhanced data rates for the global system in the mobile communication evolution.

A broader context, telecommunication covers media, broadcasting, entertainment, and recreation (Low, 2000a). With twofour54 starting in 2011, Abu Dhabi has much to catch-up in the knowledge-software part of media and broadcasting, especially those related to Arabic language and culture (El Adeb *et al.*, 2007; Emirates Centre for Strategic Studies and Research, ed, 2007b, 2008b and 2009b) in contrast to the infrastructure-hardware aspects.

3.6. Real estate, Construction Services and Business Professional Services

The sector real estate, construction services and business professional services contributed 8.4% to Abu Dhabi's GDP in 2009, the largest in the services sector (Table 2.1). The sector is set to grow with the new property law and national home ownership in motion. The Urban Planning Council's 2007 master plan (http//www.abudhabi.ae) twins with Vision 2030. An upgrading of real estate management services, facilities management and more affordable homes to large expatriate needs are identified.

Unlike Dubai's real estate bubble bursting, Abu Dhabi expects some 22,000 new housing units to be delivered in 2011, which have already started affecting demand and rentals of existing properties. Unlike mature Dubai, Abu Dhabi still has a supply gap to bridge. Over 17,000 government villas for Emiratis planned for the next five years. Its developers took a middle course not to cancel projects, but any delay would help in a credit crunch.

At the local level, the Abu Dhabi Municipality has to accelerate both regulations and enforcement to keep the aesthetics of the city in

---

[46] *Middle East Economic Digest*, August 25–31, 2006, special report on telecoms.

bold plans. Eventually it needs an enforceable strata law to enable owners' associations to manage maintenance.[47] It needs extensive reclassification, the same for a green code for buildings for energy-saving. It is a challenge in a largely expatriate society used to subsidised utilities; free for Emiratis.

The green building code aims to cut energy bills by 40% and 26% in less water use in new homes under the Urban Planning Council's Estidama Pearl Rating System. Its biggest task is to conduct mass public education and awareness programmes more than the technical training sessions for developers, engineers, architects, and others on the new rules.

More than a real estate play, a twist is shown in two Dubai propositions. One is Dubai as an entrenched *entrepôt* economy with world-class infrastructure, but mired by its pricked real estate bubble to use that as a blessing in disguise. With price correction, its next move is to offer more affordable premises in its many free zones for business incubators to attract, retain, and create jobs. Its exponential growth was pricing itself out. Now, it can revive and become competitive again by attracting entrepreneurs and talents.

The other is Emaar Properties as part of its outreach to build housing quickly and cheaply for war-ravaged Angola in exchange for a mining concession in Angola's Northwest area where diamonds, iron ore and rare minerals are in abundant. Emaar will bring business opportunities for many others in Dubai's free zones as part of the supply chain for procurement of supplies and services. It is beyond pure real estate as Dubai's next lap, allowing its revenue from fees and user charges to continue.

The remaining segment of business services, especially in consulting, legal and accounting are highly correlated to the real estate sector and financial services. Equally, there are more expatriate professionals

---

[47] Dubai was the first to have its Strata Law allowing foreigners to directly own shares of common areas in land designated as freehold, for their maintenance. Abu Dhabi's solution for foreign ownership of buildings above the land without owning the land itself is allowing homeowners' associations to control and upkeep common areas. In practice, the idea is not smooth in execution; *Gulf News*, August 28, 2010.

than Emiratis just as the real estate is as import-reliant, but of lower skilled construction workers.

Abu Dhabi is yet to have a legal professional association and an accreditation body. These seem misunderstood and confused as a nonprofit community or social body instead of benchmarks standards, quality, and best practices. A rethink is as timely of classification of building contractors and consultants purely for regulation by size of projects rather than for development of professionalism and safety.

3.7. Medical, Biotechnology and Biomedical Services

The health sector[48] looking into a medical cluster for Abu Dhabi by the General Authority on Health Services is not new. It is remade into the Health Authority Abu Dhabi. With high renal failures, the Mubadala Development Company's Imperial College London Diabetes Centre goes straight in on a needs basis.

With requisite funds, strategic partners and alliances, there is an ample base of Arabic patients and clinical records for research and development and studies for the epidemiology of diseases. New lifestyles with exercises more than diet control as prevention are part of the new culture to mitigate hereditary diseases. New medicines and curative methodologies would take as much time as changing habits.

Mindful of ethical issues such as *in vitro*-fertilisation and embryos acceptable as life forms, a 2008 federal law to license and regulate fertility centres has banned the storage of frozen embryos. It was passed, but not enforced until 2010. The law cited two *fatwas* as rulings from the Dubai Islamic Affairs and Charitable Activities Department and the Abu Dhabi Judicial Department on *in-vitro* fertilisation leading to mixed lineage.

---

[48] Primary health care is at the general practitioner level, secondary level involves specialised ambulatory medical services and hospital care (out-patient and in-patient services) often via referral from primary health care services. Tertiary level is the diagnosis and treatment of disease and disability, medical and related services involving high complexity and costs.

In 2010, by-laws of the federal law on organ transplant were approved by the UAE Health Council. It allows the bequeath of kidneys, liver, lungs, pancreas, and heart upon death to save lives. Laws continue to allow the living, mentally, and physically fit individuals over 21 years to donate life-sustaining organs.

The national donor system changes everything. Despite enactment of various laws, it takes time to train physicians, nurses and transplant teams with no heart surgeons yet in Abu Dhabi. Not all UAE hospitals are licensed for organ transplant. The Ministry of Health has the final say.

Further growth and development lie in potential of information communication technology for health care including electronic medical records, telemedicine, tele-care, patient-monitor, patient care for drug administration, sensory motion detector to trigger fall-alarm for both young and elderly; near-field for small payments as in parking also helps. But joining all the dots is a reality check.

3.8. Wealth Accumulation

In sovereign wealth funds, the Abu Dhabi Investment Authority is responsible for managing all of the government's oil revenues and assets.[49] Its first 2009 annual report adopting some of the Santiago Principles reported average annual returns of 6.5% and 8% in the 20- and 30-year, respectively to 2009. Its allocation includes stocks, bonds and other investment with 80% of its assets managed by external fund managers.

The Abu Dhabi Investment Company with a capital of $272.5 million is jointly owned by the Abu Dhabi Investment Authority (97.9%) and the National Bank of Abu Dhabi (2.1%). As a public limited liability company, its principal activities include investment and merchant banking, trade finance, portfolio management; securities and commodities trading, brokerage services and venture capital

---

[49] Anecdotal information from the news media may have the Abu Dhabi Investment Authority investing around $600 million in Apollo Management's new publicly listed fund, or 40% of the initial public offer. This is doubly unique as a big stake in a public-traded private equity firm.

investment. It specialises in providing investment and corporate finance advisory services, the first investment company to be established. Its daily trading volume is up to $2 billion.

Law No. 16 of 2006 has the Abu Dhabi Investment Council[50] replacing the Abu Dhabi Investment Authority and all its investment, seemingly a sister fund. It is tax-exempt, and it invests inside and outside of Abu Dhabi in a diversified balanced portfolio with guarantees on investment. Its investment policy includes investment and reinvestment in any capital assets or real rights, in shares and bonds, securities transactions and projects.

In 2009, the Federal National Council approved the legislation to limit the extent to which the federal government can tap into international and local debt markets. It is 45% of UAE total GDP or Dh300 billion, whichever is the smaller. At the emirate-level, the limit is 15% of the emirate's GDP to ensure that none borrows excessively. There was no plan to sell federal bonds in 2010.

3.9. Other Domestic Capital, Direct Foreign Investment and Technology Acquisition

A differentiation of inward and outward direct foreign investment is relevant. Inward direct foreign investment and multinational corporations may be drawn by government procurement contracts in Abu Dhabi or using it as an export beach-head for the region or both. Transfers of technology, knowledge and markets apply to inward and outward direct foreign investment for linkages to the global value chain and supply chain.

Both are recorded as committed investment as a leading indicator of prevailing investor confidence and realised or actual is an indicator of reality. Presence of any gap reflects changes in the business environment, some as exogenous, beyond Abu Dhabi's control. Regionness always matters in attracting investment, foreign or local.

---

[50]Abbreviated the Council, not ADIC is to be distinct from the Abu Dhabi Investment Company.

Table 3.2.   Total direct foreign investment by economic activity, 2005–2006.

Dh million	2005	2006	Growth rate %
Agriculture	197	129	−34
Mining	1,648	1,914	16
Manufacturing	5,962	9,606	16
Water, electricity	1,311	1,545	18
Construction	18,428	19,879	8
Wholesale, retail	8,489	9,587	13
Restaurants, hotels	53	88	65
Transport, storage, communication	2,784	3,460	24
Finance, insurance	21,755	23,583	8
Other	1,283	1,535	20

Source: UAE Ministry of Economy, 2006, p. 13.

Apart from annual UNDP World Investment Reports (http://www.unctad.org and Al Jaber 2008) reporting at a country-level, one UAE data source is by Ministry of Economy.[51] With UAE Central Bank, balance of payments data, the first and only survey in 2005 survey was initiated to track direct foreign investment.

Finance and insurance took the biggest share of direct foreign investment in 2005 and 2006, followed by construction (Table 3.2). This suggests that capital formation is more in machinery and equipment for construction than productive industries. Dubai led in both years with Dh37,435 million in 2005 and Dh42,463 million in 2006 at 13% growth rate. Abu Dhabi's respective figures were Dh15,430 million and Dh16,171 million at 5%.

By source, Japan accounted for 20.6% and 22.0%, respectively in 2005 and 2006; the UK 20.3% and 24.6%, respectively, both

---

[51]The national team comprises the Central Bank and others in economic development and investment, municipalities and chambers of commerce with a list of enterprises from the Ministry of Labour and technical assistance from the United Nations. Survey forms elicit information on real and comprehensive direct foreign investment data, its types, sources, motives, challenges and impact to contribute to UAE companies and economy at large; UAE Central Bank and Ministry of Economy, various years.

combined as over 40% as major investors. China is a potential. Exports and employment from manufacturing dominated in both years. While the UAE is attractive for stability, location and costs, 72.6% of respondents put high operation cost including fuel cost as a constraint for energy-intensive industries.

Statistics for Abu Dhabi's domestic investment and direct foreign investment are lacking. Media *report put it as the second most attractive city in the Middle East for direct foreign investment in* 2010.[52] While not dependent on the capital *per se*, direct foreign investment is a catalyst to diversify GDP and boost private sector maturity.

Sovereign wealth funds, notably, Mubadala Development Company is diversified to lead. Their dual bottom-lines in commercial-social profit takes them to the developing and emerging states for commodities, alternative investments and financial services firms, not just OECD iconic deals since the global financial crisis. Seeming in oil, International Petroleum Investment Company in 2010 took a 4.99% stake in Italy's Unicredit and with its subsidiary Aabar Investments, they hold a 9.1% stake Daimler and Mercedes-Benz.

Beside privatisation, Abu Dhabi also taps public–private partnerships (Department of Planning and Economy, 2008) as in build-operate-transfer and other hybrids. The Abu Dhabi Water and Electricity Authority remains the pioneer with a full range of privatisation and public–private partnerships for power and gas. The typical pattern is a government monopoly or state-owned enterprise to first commercialise the government assets. Then an initial public offer is to inject capital. If more capital is needed to support the operator, then it becomes a strategic investment.

Zonescorp has public–private partnerships for its Industrial City of Abu Dhabi in Musaffah and Al Ain and worker residential cities as the government basically owns and supplies the land. The Sheikh Khalifa Medical City is in a public–private partnership with Cleveland Hospital in a management contract to run its hospital and facilities.

---

[52] Despite the Arab Spring or in spite of it as Abu Dhabi, Qatar and Dubai are deemed politically stable and relatively safe havens in their respective rights; *Financial Times*, March 30, 2011.

Since 2006, the Abu Dhabi Education Council with CfBT, the UK education trust have been in public–private partnerships using some 700 expert advisers and licensed teachers to support schools participating in the New School Model.[53] At the end of the three-year partnership, the experts are leaving, having supported an initial of 30 schools in a pilot for 116 of 180 Abu Dhabi schools. The schools are ready to take over and continue.

Less successful is the Department of Transport using a public–private partnership as build-operate-transfer for the Mafraq-Ghweifat Highway.[54] With the contractors claiming a lack of understanding of the concept, they also warn of setbacks to other big projects if the highway partnership was scrapped. Apparently stalled by the high cost, the highway may be too big for an initial foray into an infrastructure public–private partnership.

Apart from lacking the economic and technical knowledge in fully tapped all forms of direct foreign investment, there remains a gap in the understanding of value chain, supply chain and Porter's five-forces as a competitive advantage. A resulting resistance to the foreign investors by the local investors is more is the pity given ample, abundant funds to promote both instead of needless rivalry. It is not an unusual perception in economic development for local private sector which feels neglected.

As remiss is a good communication and awareness programme marketing Vision 2030 thoroughly and intensively across all sectors, segments of the community and society, regions and stakeholders. Except for Abu Dhabi Inc with enlightened leadership in the national champions, the local private sector is naturally fearful of their protection being jeopardised as foreign entry is welcomed by Vision 2030.

---

[53] Under the New School Model, two head teachers managing two languages Arabic and English are in Grades 1–12 classrooms at the same time with a new curriculum. Longer working days for teachers and compulsory training programmes are for all teachers; *The National,* May 18, 2011.

[54] This extends the Mafraq Highway to Al Ghweifat as a new 327 kilometre highway to Saudi Arabia, costing Dh10 billion or $2.72 billion over three-year as a test case; *The National,* May 18 and 24, 2011.

If that perception in manufacturing is persistent, then it is stronger in knowledge-based services which are more alien to traditional, conservative small firms, except entrepreneurial younger start-ups. Work attitude and culture are visceral and need sensitivity in remoulding not merely as neutral modern technology inputs. This is where the enabling factors come in to make necessary changes in such scenarios (explanation follows in Chapter 4).

Chapter 4

ENABLERS IN LABOUR, LAWS AND REGULATIONS

4.1. Introduction

Economic development mobilises various factors such as land, labour, and capital to generate national output and income. The remaining enabling factor, in this chapter, pertains to human resources (Emirates Centre for Strategic Studies and Research, ed, 2010b; United Nations Development Programme, 2010) in terms of education (Wiseman, 2011; Kirk, 2010; Emirates Centre for Strategic Studies and Research, ed, 2010c) and labour as derived from population. This chapter rounds up empirical evidence on both quantity and quality of human capital, including welfare and social security.

Previous chapters have shown that Abu Dhabi has abundant land and hydrocarbon generating resources, and resulting wealth as capital, but lacks in human resources development. In particular, it is a two-fold challenge, one as education and continuous education and training for skills upgrading in the pre- and post-employment situations, respectively. The other side of the coin has population as destiny; a small base and a large migrant labour pool along with issues of emiratisation and national identity.

Finally, the right set of laws and regulations in a harsher global trading system (Petri *et al.*, 2007) is required to combine all the factors of economic development together to deliver Vision 2030. Abu Dhabi has no deficit in laws, just the laborious time-consuming process of amending and modifying or introducing new laws that are aligned to the UAE's international agreements and protocols for the 21st century. Enforcement is another matter, either missing or poor.

4.2. Human Capital Formation and Human Resources Development

The puzzle of noncoincidence of economic development and human resources development (United Nations Development Programme, 2010) is neither new nor unique to Abu Dhabi. There are diverse paths to progress even among high-income countries. Some countries become top performers on the UNDP Human Development Index, not by only relying on the basis of economic growth, but because of their exceptional progress in health and education sectors.

Economic and income growth provide the financial wherewithal. Yet, the existence of well-educated women does not automatically mean that they will join the labour force. A surprisingly weak correlation between GDP growth and indicators of health and education is partly due to the long, variable lags in translating GDP wealth into human capital outcomes. Partly too, other non-income factors like innovations in medicine, democratising and decentralising education are more directly causal.

Quintessentially, population and immigration go together; the latter as a buffer has become too big a tail wagging the head. This default position is unintended, without a longer-term population policy. A two-fold stress is Emirati human capital formation and human resources development; and a labour and employment policy upgrading the labour pool dominated by expatriates. Any division is artificial. Substitution of Emiratis for low-skilled non-nationals is neither desirable nor sustainable in many high-skilled jobs.

Once a clear population-immigration policy emerges,[1] without the UAE ready to go as far as offering permanent residency

---

[1]A Federal Council for Demographic Structure by a higher committee for a visionary blueprint and time line for implementation is being sent to the federal cabinet for approval, with no details except for some emiratisation plans for sectors like aviation; *The National*, April 2, 2011.

status[2] (Goujon *et al.*, 2010), a review of Abu Dhabi[3] statistics of population and demography is to see the challenge and response. A six-fold rise between 1975 and 2005, reaching 1.4 million by census data, was estimated at 1.6 million by mid-2009, comprising 24.8% nationals and 75.2% non-nationals.

Despite falling growth rates and fertility rates as typically observed in many educated women at work, a youthful age structure has 40.2% of nationals below age 15, 57.6% aged 15–64 and 2.2% aged 65 and over. The average annual population growth rate between 1995 and 2005 for nationals at 4.53% is bigger than for non-nationals at 3.77% for the same period. This shows that it is a political decision to balance labour, demography, and national identity with migrant inflow since 2005.

Once the political direction for population is clear for Vision 2030 with a quality-oriented emiratisation policy, the resultant immigration policy is in tandem with a manpower-cum-education plan. Human capital formation for Emiratis is both education and continuous education and training for new technology per science, technology and innovation policy. It is imperative that all these elements have policy coherence.

Putting nationals at the centre first, stepwise and priority-wise means remaining human resources development falls on the immigration policy as a buffer. With an existing pool of largely unskilled foreign labour, it is another political decision to stop further inflow of more of the same. Instead, gearing new migrants by strict criteria in education, skills and qualities suited to the trio of manpower and education plans and science, technology and innovation policy is imperative.

The existing pool of unskilled can be selectively weaned by natural attrition such as by not renewing visas on expiry, and identifying those to retain for skills upgrading. Sponsorship remains with more flexibility to change jobs.[4] The residency and work visas are aligned to two-year,

---

[2]Qatar is considering permanent residency for expatriates with pre-determined criteria, in line with Qatar National Development Strategy 2011–2016 to attract and retain highly skilled labour, *inter alia* review, revise the sponsorship system and set up a tribunal resolve labour disputes; *The National*, March 29, 2011.
[3]All statistics and information are from the Statistics Centre Abu Dhabi.
[4]Previously, once a contract or job is terminated, the worker and all dependents have to leave the UAE. Another job needs another sponsor. More flexibly, all can remain while

not three-year for residency. At the federal level, the criteria and visa structure for Property Investor Residence Visas are amended and tightened.[5]

While logical and neat, these pieces in the architecture of human resources development need equally committed policies and enforcement to stay on course. Vision 2030 is a default timeframe for reform. It takes time to reform the education system from primary, secondary, technical, vocational to tertiary in order to resolve the education-skill mismatch.

It takes longer to change mindset involving traditions, values, and customs. The young may be easier to convince relative to their parents. Even teachers need to be retrained. All learning organisations enable continuous education and training, including self-learning.

The trio of plans emphasise science and mathematics. There are two global benchmarks. The forerunner is the Programme for International Student Assessment examinations assessing the levels of mathematics, science and literacy of 15-year-olds; Finnish students topped in the last round in 2010. Another is the International Association for the Evaluation of Educational Achievement's Trends in International Mathematics and Science Study since 1995.[6] Singapore[7] and increasingly China topped the trends.[8]

---

a new sponsor is processed with the requisite fees and conditions. The UAE will not scrap the sponsorship system as Kuwait and Bahrain did, on grounds of sovereignty.
[5]Dubai started the trend in its property boom without clarity in laws until now; *The National*, June 8, 2011.
[6]This holds competitions to assess mathematics and science achievement of students in the third, fourth, seventh and eighth grades, and in the final year of secondary school.
[7]Singapore schools have adopted since 2001 a mathematics teaching programme, called HeyMath htpp://www.heymath.com, to teach mathematics in an unconventional, but practical and play format. It was developed in Chennai, India by two Indian bankers in partnership with the Millennium Mathematics Project at the Cambridge University. A team of Indian, British, and Chinese education specialists produced the best practices in animation tools, delivered on the Internet for any mathematics teacher from any part of the world to adopt or adapt.
[8]Dubai's Knowledge and Human Development Authority began to make comparisons. It is timely with the new curriculum by India's Central Board of Secondary Education-International (CBSE-i) in place, focusing on science and mathematics; *Khaleej Times*, June 23, 2010 and May 26, 2010.

The Abu Dhabi Education Council is switching public schools to a Finnish curriculum[9] after introducing an Australian-based curriculum in 2006. The Council unveiled its Higher Education Strategic Plan in 2010, in collaboration with the UAE University and Advanced Technology Investment Company's Ecosystem Development.

Four priorities for higher education includes raising quality to internationally recognised levels; aligning to social, cultural, and economic needs; building and maintaining a research eco-system to drive an innovation-based economy; and provide all qualified students with affordable access to higher education.[10]

The average 2010 scores in the UAE Common Educational Proficiency Assessment examination for admission to federal universities for Abu Dhabi remain constant. It is no higher than any other emirate. Beside joint examinations for admission, the UAE University, Zayed University[11] and Higher Colleges of Technology in various emirates have allowed transfers by Emirati students for courses and institutes of their choice after standardising the foundation courses in mathematics and English.[12]

---

[9] This is as part of a partnership between the Abu Dhabi Education Council and a Finnish firm, EduCluster; *The National*, June 14, 2010.

[10] Each priority is delivered by flagship strategic initiatives, measured by set target metrics, all developed by the higher education taskforce since 2009 comprising local institutions, Harvard Business School, Oxford University, Imperial College London; *The National*, June 10, 2010.

[11] The Emirates Foundation for Philanthropy gave a Dh16 million Sheikh Mohammed bin Zayed Higher Education Grant programme for enabling graduates from Zayed University (1998, first federal university for women) graduates to advance their studies locally and abroad. Priority fields include education, social studies; tourism, museum, curatorial studies; healthcare, public administration; environment and engineering; aeronautics and astronautics; and nuclear engineering and management; *The National*, May 18, 2011.

[12] These remedial courses run until reforms at lower levels are successful. Joint application is via the National Assessment and Placement Office with a Common Educational Proficiency Assessment score of less than 160 points going to Higher Colleges of Technology to imply more demand for its foundation courses. Then more places will be in demand at the other two universities. A score of five is needed for the International English Language Testing System score for degree courses; *The National*, May 25, 2011.

Many new private universities have been set up in Abu Dhabi, mostly in partnerships with foreign ones, including Masdar Institute, INSEAD, New York University Abu Dhabi for Humanities, Khalifa University for Science and Technology, Abu Dhabi University and Sorbonne University. Some of these institutions will ultimately be located on the Saadiyat Island. The world-renowned, branded ones are well-endowed,[13] but they carry the risk of not delivering their mandate if there is a deficit of local students.[14]

Other than funding and the lure of the region despite the 2011 Arab Spring, there is no known market size by disciplines. Vision 2030 guides only by sectors. Branding goes both ways. Exceptionally wealthy, ambitious Abu Dhabi, especially male students go West to the parent campuses for a truly multicultural campus life. But home-bound women may be tapped.

Reforms continue to tackle the high 22% school drop outs, especially Emirati males aged 20–24 years (Emirates Centre for Strategic Studies and Research, ed, 2011) blamed on uninspiring school environments, lack of interest, subject options, student counselling and ease of getting job without qualifications, including the police and armed forces. Alternatives to academic education are recognised as in the Petroleum Institute.

To balance regional economic development, in parallel with Khalifa Fund going into the Western Region or Al Gharbia in the Abu Dhabi emirate, Northern and Eastern Emirates, it seems timely to build the missing middle level of vocational technicians in the manpower pyramid.

---

[13] The New York University Abu Dhabi's model as revealed seems similar to Masdar Institute's student intake of mainly foreigners with similar issues including keeping high-calibre faculty in Abu Dhabi or adversely affecting their brands by being abroad; *The International Herald Tribune*, April 15, 2011.

[14] Michigan State University in Dubai since 2008 closed its undergraduate courses in 2010. It is trying to rebuild by diversifying into postgraduate master's degrees from public health, car safety to obesity; *The National*, May 18, 2011. George Mason University was the first American school in Ras Al Khaimah in 2007, exiting in 2010 without graduating a single student. Indian University of Pune exited in 2011 from Ras Al Khaimah free zone despite its 2011 intake of 54 as the biggest and 72 cumulative students since 2006. It relocated, but it is not accredited by Ministry of Higher Education and Scientific Research.

Diplomas are stigmatised, but may be a route, topping up to university degrees.

The Institute of Applied Technology formed in 2005 by a royal degree is a world-class career-technical education system for scientists, engineers, and technicians in six institutes in pursuit of Vision 2030. The Abu Dhabi Polytechnic established in 2010 offers a dual educational-professional training system with multiple high-technology specialised disciplines for technologists, engineers, and industrial manpower for Vision 2030. It also offers two higher diploma programmes in nuclear and semiconductor technology. The Institute of Applied Technology-Kaplan is for English, aviation, health sciences, and logistics.

The Vocational Education Development Centre is a boarding institute catering for Emiratis who have an interest in vocational studies rather than mainstream academic education. Al Ain International Aviation Academy aims to be a leading Middle East specialised aviation educational establishment in the Middle East and emiratisation of aerospace careers.

Established in 2006, Fatima College of Health Sciences is for skilled healthcare professionals leading to a Bachelor of Nursing degree and other specialisations in allied health and public health in the near future.

The Vocational Education and Training Institute since 2007 offers 3-year diploma courses in business, design, information technology and services (travel, tourism, library science, finance) in Abu Dhabi, Al Ain and Madinat Zayed in Al Gharbia. With about 1,000 students, it is marketing its diplomas to jobless Emiratis as a start.

Separately, the Institute of Applied Technology and Khalifa University of Science, Technology and Research signed a memorandum of understanding in 2011. It launched an Advanced Science programme to upgrade outstanding students at the institute to become part of the first batch at Faculty of Medicine at Khalifa University.

In telecommunication, Abu Dhabi's Etisalat BT Innovation Centre housed in Khalifa University is inspired by insects' vast labyrinthine nests to do nature-inspired computing.[15] There is certainly

---

[15] Wireless networks use a lot of power, so algorithms switch off networks when not used, relocating power to others at peak times for network efficiency. Computers can run faster with fibre-optics, mobile health, data management and technologies for smartphones; *The National*, February 5 2011.

a lot of nature in Al Gharbia[16] to explore with the right education and talents.

4.3. Labour and Employment Policy

4.3.1. *Emirati labour*

Full employment[17] of all nationals takes time as different work cultures and mindsets have to be dealt with. As more Emiratis seek higher education, they can be more demanding and choosy. The right kind of work attitude comes with skills and knowledge. No matter how the data are presented, the root problem in any labour and employment policy lies in the high voluntary unemployment of nationals. It is a paradox, contradiction or irony despite emiratisation and a pure passive reliance on migrant labour.

The economics of unemployment of nationals at 12% in evidence-based studies (McCrohan *et al.*, 2009; Mercator Fund and International Council on Security and Development, 2011; Forstenlechner *et al.*, 2010a, 2010b, 2011) are beset with socioeconomic-cultural issues. It needs brave and strong policies. On one hand, male Emiratis in the oil sector, armed forces and police are gaining skills and professional degrees and qualifications at respective institutes. On the other hand, women, even though they are well educated with university degrees, remain unemployed or unemployable by choice or culture.

A low women labour force participation rate is due to less mobility to go to where jobs are, without part-time options and flexibility of labour laws for pension and social security benefits. A sequestered wealth

---

[16] Oil-rich Al Gharbia has 40% of Abu Dhabi's GDP. It will house facilties in renewable energy, from solar to nuclear facilities; *The National*, February 5, 2011.

[17] Full employment is a sum of frictional and structural employment, the latter rising over time with ageing and new technology displacing, especially older and less educated workers. The Phillips curve as an inverse relationship between the rates of inflation and unemployment with an equilibrating non-accelerating inflation rate of unemployment seems irrelevant as a policy tradeoff in the UAE with free-flowing labour.

of human capital including the early retirees[18] can be unleashed for mid-career paths (Critchley, 2002, 2006). Khalifa Fund cannot be serving a nanny state. It needs creative innovations to mobilise jobless Emiratis.

It is not just women Emiratis who shy away from the multicultural private sector. Less traditional banking, insurance and hospitality sectors are shunned, be it cultural or religious. The usual preference for public sector jobs is aided and abetted by better pay, working hours, public holidays, leave, total job security and stability. As a minority, it is comforting to be in government jobs, around other Emiratis sharing a work culture and understanding as in unconditional priority for family.

Private sector conditions are criticised, but not rejected. The more enlightened Emiratis are open to a need to learn, adapt, and accept other work cultures. More incentives include augmented subsidised pay. Better yet are role models, especially of successful Emiratis. They exist in family business, small and medium-sized enterprises and start-ups via the Khalifa Fund. Convincing parents, guardians, supportive employers and colleagues can make the private sector a more compelling value proposition.

More than treating the symptoms, the root causes of voluntary unemployment and shunning private sector jobs have to be mitigated resolutely. Overall, the Ministry of Labour estimated some 200,000 Emiratis joining the labour force in a decade.[19] It has 35,000 unemployed Emiratis, curiously including those working, but looking for another job which falls to 10,000 of the retired looking for work; unemployment is voluntary. [20]

---

[18] A proposal to lower retirement rate for females to 35 years is mindful of their dual roles, economically and biologically.

[19] Emiratis and foreign workers on visas issued by the Ministry of Labour can move around emirates, except for other regulation of respective free zones; *The National*, May 8, 2011.

[20] Unemployment is conventionally defined as those not holding a job, but looking for work as part of the labour supply as economically active (ages 15 to 65) with other employed. The economically inactive as not in the workforce are the retired, those studying and home-workers; *Gulf News*, May 8, 2011 and *Khaleej Times*, May 16, 2011.

Most of the unemployed are in the southern parts in Fujairah and Khor Fakkan. Bringing work-to-workers, rather than workers-to-work needs the right industries to match skills and other economic conditions to support emiratisation. They are not necessarily traditional or cottage industries. New capabilities via vocational institutes bring a range of possibilities to the deserts and rural parts.

More Emiratis in private sector jobs start with more thoughtful internships in Emirati family-owned firms which groom their successors over the generations. Self-selective nationals voluntarily opt for the extra hardship and sacrifice to learn new skills in the private sector as an engine of growth. It is more than the minimum wages[21] and other state-supplemented incentives.

How Emiratis are challenged into the dynamism and vibrancy of knowledge-intensive careers need a more thoughtful process than lamenting mismatched skills. In parallel, stereotyped perceptions of Emiratis among foreign employers, supervisors, line managers and other multicultural staff need to be revised.

Public sector work is more administrative and regulatory. Job security and upward mobility may reach a glass ceiling. Initiatives should be taken to design the work environment by some imaginative crowd-sourcing, such as community-based soliciting for suggestions can assess the expectations of Emiratis with regard to balancing work and home. Private sector jobs can be stable, secure, conducive to family responsibilities and more.

Realistically, all know that profitability and productivity matter in the world of risks and uncertainty as Abu Dhabi globalises. The right management can encourage Emiratis to take the road less travelled for skills and knowledge. The initial years are the hardest, but if treated as an extension of learning, Emiratis are empowered.

It may be an oversimplification, but culturally emotive and visceral Emiratis can adapt to 21st century work life as they easily adopt high technology culture-neutral cars and mobile phones. Such modernity,

---

[21] A monthly minimum wage is set at Dh5,000 for post-secondary Emirati school certificate holders, Dh4,000 for secondary school certificate holders and Dh3,000 for those below secondary.

competition, profit-motivation underpin creativity and innovation to be posed as a challenge to the aspiring youths rather than as a threat. With help available, owning their business have unlimited blue-sky opportunities.

4.3.2. *Foreign labour*

The overwhelming pool of non-nationals seems to reflect no explicit immigration policy by work criteria. By tradition, Zayed's humanitarian philosophy freely allowed families and dependents. The second generation of children know more about Abu Dhabi than their native homes. Up to a point, these second-generation educated youths can be harnessed as skilled labour without much additional cost with proper accreditation.

On who pays for skills upgrading and human resources development of the existing foreign labour pool, Singapore employers since 1979 pay a mandatory skills development fund levy.[22] Bahrain's Human Resources Development Fund in 2004 has optional contributions from the firms. Critical skills are more than on-the-job training especially for emerging sectors. Poaching is averted as training is tied to sponsors as employers.

Abu Dhabi is generally constructive in its foreign worker policy. Zonescorp's worker residential cities in Musaffah and Al Ain are replicated elsewhere with health testing of potential foreign labour in their home countries before arrival. The Tourism Development and Investment Company is addressing the remaining issues on human rights (Van Esveld, 2009; Hadi, 2006) in its Saadiyat projects.[23]

The Ministry of Labour has simplified the registration process with e-government including foreign worker payment system by

---

[22] Singapore's Central Provident Fund is beyond old age social security with housing, education, medical, and investment schemes; (Low, 2000b; Low *et al.*, 2004b).
[23] Human Rights Watch has some 130 artists including many in the Middle East to boycott Guggenheim Museum Abu Dhabi. PricewaterhouseCoopers has been appointed as a watchdog with regular audits and interviews for the welfare of some 20,000 workers on Saadiyat Island; *International Herald Tribune*, March 16, 2011 and *The National*, June 1, 2011.

Table 4.1. The social cost of labour in the UAE.

	%/Dh		
	Skilled	Unskilled	Average
Ratio to total %	19.5	80.5	Na
Recruitment cost	3,404	2,296	2,674
Wages and non-cash benefits	129,302	18,925	41,000
Social cost*	14,066	14,066	14,066
Fees	−2,507	−2,507	−2,507
Total cost	144,265	32,780	55,233
Productivity	490,792	141,831	212,162

*Every foreigner costs Dh14,066 per annum, of which the firm pays Dh2,506 in fees and social cost forms about 20% of the total cost of workers.
Source: Reported in *Gulf News*, October 13, 2010.

banks for timely payments. It mandated summer mid-day breaks. For labour mobility, it removed the six-month ban and no-objection-certificate and raised the retirement age for foreigners from 60 to 65 years.[24]

Permits for part-time work are the first in the region. Resident visas and labour cards cut from three to two years drew mixed reactions, but are generally in the right direction to rein in reliance on migrant labour.

The Ministry of Labour and Zayed University's study in 2010 shows that it costs Dh50 billion per annum to host 4 million foreigners in the UAE (Tables 4.1 and 4.2).

The UAE Labour Force Survey 2009[25] reiterated that relying on cheap unskilled labour is no longer in line with the vision for future growth. The central question is how to unify an understanding of economic development for the government's vision to create the diverse knowledge-based economy. Ensuring more Emirati contribution and upgrading skills across-the-board needs a global talent policy.

---

[24] Like professionals since January 2011, foreigners with secondary education in manual jobs can move if paid monthly a minimum wage of Dh5,000, Dh7,000 for diploma, Dh12,000 for bachelor's degree, with residence visa stamped; *Gulf News*, December 9, 2010 and *The National*, June 21, 2011.
[25] *Gulf News*, October 13, 2010.

Table 4.2.   Breakdown of subsidies per annum.

Subsidies	Dh
Electricity subsidies	6,466
Security cost	4,382
Fuel subsidies	1,204
Road and transportation	209
Health	932
Education	378
Total	14,066

Source: As in Table 4.1.

On the other side of the coin literally, remittances are a lifesaver[26] as humanitarian petrodollars recycling. Despite the Arab Spring, GCC remittances were estimated at $74.9 billion in 2011 and $65.6 billion in 2010.[27] Another guesstimate in 2009 is remittances from the Arab Gulf states by some to 13 million workers averaged at $60 billion per year with $338 billion globally in 2008. The International Association of Money Transfer Networks puts the UAE is the world's third-largest source of remittances.

A rough rule of the thumb shows a 1% point growth in real GDP growth raising GDP growth rate of workers' countries of origin by 1.3% point. Adding remittances, official development assistance, direct foreign investment in acquisition of assets abroad, Abu Dhabi as a capital exporter mitigated the effects of the global financial crisis at its peak in 2008/2009. Both the first and third worlds know Abu Dhabi now.

---

[26] Liwa Street in Abu Dhabi is the unofficial remittance district of *hawala* and money changers. Innovative field agents as smaller currency brokers provide a value-added service. *Kebayaran* or compatriot Filipinos collect, hold on to remittances until better exchange rates at the *hawala* to send money home. They visit customers in the labour camps or worker residential cities, nurses in hospitals or hairdressers in shops. Housemaids in their employers' homes may put as little as Dh100 under doormats, to be picked up and left with handwritten receipts. The extended *hawala* network of currency agents ferries sums back to Liwa Street as a triple win for customers, intermediaries and *hawala* based on trust and low transaction cost.

[27] *Gulf News*, May 1, 2011 and February 23, 2010.

4.4. Emiratisation, Family Business, Small and Medium-Sized Enterprises

Abu Dhabi is unapologetic for emiratisation; Emiratis being a minority at home. It is not what, but how. Quotas decreed by timeframes started with banking in 1998 at 4% quota accumulated (presumably of total workforce), then insurance in 2003 at 5% and trading companies with more than 50 employees in 2008 at 2%, rising to 3% for 50–200 employees and 4% for over 200 employees[28] (http://www. hrdc.ae/emiratisation, Mashood *et al.*, undated). The education sector is fully emiratised in Arabic teaching.

Banking and insurance sectors are deemed as professional and high-skilled. Moving to professions, a 2005 ministerial decision required the emiratisation of public relations officers or government relations officers who liaise between firms and the government. It was extended in 2006 for secretarial and human resources managerial positions. Most unemployed nationals are young secondary school holders. The majority is female.

Progress is slow and poor. Some backsliding or slippage in the banks is despite more branches opened. The Ministry of Labour has penalties including termination of transactions for unfulfilled quotas. As new labour laws generally raise labour, and hence business cost, a tiered system of fees for labour cards[29] is extended from the mid-2011 deadline to the end-2011. More multicultural firms by the diversity of staff, pay less.

Skilled workers are defined as those with university degrees. If Emiratis are 15% of 20% of total skilled workers, then firms pay Dh300 per foreign labour card. It is Dh600 if no single nationality accounts

---

[28] One national with special needs equates two nationals without special needs. New quotas by Saudi labour ministry seem harsher; Nitaqat (Ranges) programme by September 2011 determines firms by sector of activity and size to be entitled to employ foreigners depending on performance in abiding by quotas: Banks up to 500 staff with at least 49% Saudis, wholesale trade same staff size, minimum 19%, same quota to media, insurance and government schools; *Khaleej Times*, June 12, 2011 and *The National*, June 13, 2011.

[29] *The National*, 7 February, 2011 and June 6, 2011.

for more than a quarter of the workforce; Dh1,500 between a quarter and half, and Dh2,000 if over half. Failure to pay wages on time or breaking any labour laws mean a fine of Dh5,000 plus black points which are cleared annually or in six-months via remedial changes.

Firms are classified based on the following criteria: Ability-to-pay and allowing them to opt to deviate if they prefer a more culturally diversified workforce in different sectors. The flexible signals are clear if enforcement is as self-compliant by carrot-and-stick in a societal emiratisation in one fell swoop raising awareness to all. The greater good needs changes in attitude, skills, and knowledge (ASK). Mindset change is a harder imperative.

An ideal focus on quality and meritocracy blends realistically with relation-based *wasta*. It is an equally cultural DNA to be creative, not destroyed, similar to *quanxi* in the bamboo network of overseas Chinese. Both trust and lower transaction cost of relation-based connections are weighed in a globalised context against rule-based corporate governance for accountability and transparency.

There is no lack of support for Emiratis in a range of institutions and schemes. The Federal Human Resources Authority and Emirates Council for Emiratisation or Tanmia since 2002 offers training and job placement. More dedicated are Abu Dhabi's array geared to Vision 2030.

The UAE Academy established under the Abu Dhabi Chamber of Commerce and Industry trains Emiratis for private sector jobs. Its 28-week programme prepares graduates and diploma-holders. The following are taught in English — skills development, business and information technology, advice for careers, preparation of resumes, skills for interviews, team work and other self development with internship and placement. The UAE Academy is upgrading with its Abu Dhabi School of Management by 2012.

The Abu Dhabi Emiratisation (Tawteen) Council formed in 2005, spearheads the government's efforts in Emirati workforce development. It introduces Emirati job seekers to Abu Dhabi employers or firms. Training providers include UAE Academy, Higher Colleges of Technology for work readiness and Abu Dhabi University's Tawteen plan.

Since 2006, the Khalifa Fund rebranded for enterprise development has step-by-step initiatives. It has the Shell-Intillaqa training programme comprising schemes for planning (Khuta), beginning (Bedaya), growth (Zeyeda) and manufacturing (Tasnea). It even offers ideas for entrepreneurs over and above their own to apply with business plans. After interviews, they are given a business idea and finance to achieve it.

In particular, the Tasnea industrial finance scheme in 2010[30] posted job vacancies scouting for budding Emirati entrepreneurs to head up to 10 projects. Ideas among 50 Tasnea "teaser" projects include production of adhesive tape, aluminium foil containers and baby bottles to develop the plastics and metals sectors. Emirates Steel and Abu Dhabi Basic Industries would provide the raw materials. Khalifa Fund aims to fund at least 20 industrial projects yearly; Tasnea straddles between the old and new Vision 2030.

Manufacturing has a longer gestation period, needs patience in capital and profit. To grow from 7% of GDP (Table 2.1) to 25% by 2030, linking Khalifa Fund's supporting industries with bigger firms follows Porter's five-forces for competitive advantage (Fig. 1.2). Its loan financing cap, set at Dh10 million or 20% of a financing agreement encourages entrepreneurs to invest 10% as their own equity or "some skin". It is the right industrial culture to avert free-riding and moral hazard or excessive risk-taking.

Khalifa Fund's doubled capital in 2011 to Dh2 billion is UAE-wide for regional balance. Home-based Sougha projects spread entrepreneurship to rural areas. Handmade items are for domestic consumption or tourist souvenirs. Qudwa is in association with the University of Chicago Business Alumni Club whose members offer guidance, advice, counselling, experience, training in administrative and technical skills to minimise the risk of failure.

A critical mass of small and medium-sized enterprises in emerging fields, more than traditional retail or franchises of global brands would need a second board for initial public offers and ways to tap capital markets. Beside the Khalifa Fund, commercial banks have a

---

[30] Khalifa Fund extended 60 loans in 2010, by end 2010, it loans for 240 projects cumulatively, total value of Dh415 million, attracted only two Tasnea projects; *The National*, February 7 and 9, 2011.

role in financing industrial and commercial projects of small and medium-sized enterprises as noted.

The National Bank of Abu Dhabi has launched its business rent finance for short-term loans for both UAE nationals and expatriates.[31] It has joined the Emirates Islamic Bank, a subsidiary of Emirates National Bank of Dubai to finance small start-ups for all nationalities from asset-based loans to working capital finance.

Both the parent and subsidiary Emirates Banks are already financing Emirati entrepreneurs at zero-interest rate. This is via the Al Tomooh scheme, run by the Mohammed Bin Rashid Establishment for SME Development, Dubai's[32] equivalent of Khalifa Fund. The Emirates Islamic Bank offers finance to small and medium-sized enterprises with a two-year trading and financial track record. It wants such loans as 15% of its total loan portfolio.

Inter-emirate bank tie-up for small and medium-sized enterprises reflects the evolving trend of Abu Dhabi and Dubai working as a duo observed for mega projects like aluminium. More opportunities are for downstream activities. Banks' emphasis on commercial start-ups is opportune and timely to move away from pure speculative real estate assets into sustainable innovation business for entrepreneurs across all emirates.

All the institutions, funds and training resources cannot treat the symptoms without resolving the root causes. Entrepreneurship as risk-taking means success comes with failure, but coordination is to avert overlapping or more of the same given without lessons learnt. A high probability of success is in targeting home-based women as

---

[31] The loan covers rent up to Dh500,000 repaid over a period of up to one year with minimum fees. Other services include business credit card with no annual fee for up to 50 days interest-free grace period; travel insurance up to $150,000; pre-set limits on individual cards; access to cash; consolidated payments; special offers; discounts; card offer credit limit from Dh20,000–500,000; dedicated business banking centres in ZonesCorp cities, Al Ain and Jebel Ali; *The National*, May 15, 2011.

[32] Separately, Dubai's Department of Economic Development's agency, SME Dubai has its SME 100 Initiative which signed a partnership agreement with Emirates National Bank of Dubai, the first bank to offer benefits to the top 100 SMEs; *Khaleej Times*, June 7, 2011.

better educated and wanting to join the 21st century with the right products and branding.

Communication is needed to explain and market Vision 2030. Face-to-face mentoring is more than customer-centric service to guarantee understanding to translate ideas into action. Emiratis with the passion and desire to brand Abu Dhabi are nascent to be discovered. In time, they can be the next set of trainers for more entrepreneurs. It bears repeating that it is not the young Emiratis who need the selling, but their families and the community at large. They work, live and belong to the same networks.

A few case-studies of family-owned enterprises are illuminating. A small-sized enterprise is Mega doll, owned by 23-year old Mohammed Abedin.[33] Launched from his bedroom without a *fil* spent on marketing, a young entrepreneur organised an urban art exhibition in 2010 in Dubai. As a form of crowd-sourcing,[34] he displayed work from 100 local artists who doodled, painted, or sketched on the white faceless doll. A loan from the Khalifa Fund for four years, repayable only from the second year was a great help.

Creating 100-brand ambassadors also displayed on Twitter and Facebook, he was quickly contacted by small retailers and galleries, with confidence to contact Virgin Megastore which bought 900 dolls to sell in Dubai and another 1,000 in the GCC. Virgin store hosted weekly events of painting sessions with televised support in a partnership to launch a Middle East-wide competition to market the doll with the

---

[33] A 20-centimetre doll with a disproportionately big head, robot-like ears and a slouched posture reminiscent of a grumpy teenager is a good fit for the Virgin young, trendy customer base. His website, foo-dog.com develops consulting services and sells a Mega clothing range; *The National*, February 2, 2011.

[34] Open source crowd-sourcing as frugal innovation is like Wikipleadia user-generated content as a business model. Crowd-sourcing is outsourcing tasks, traditionally performed by an individual employee or contractor, to an undefined, big group of people or community (crowd) through an open call. As distributed community-based participatory design with crowd-voicing, a text-messaging software collects, then broadcast information is combined with frugal innovation. It is not just about redesigning cheaper products. It involves rethinking an entire production processes and business model to squeeze cost, make tougher products, reach more customers and accept thin profit margins to gain volume as truly knowledge-based.

winner featured on the Film and Comic Conference at the Abu Dhabi National Exhibition Centre.

A well-established family-owned conglomerate is Bin Salem Holding (http://www.binsalem.ae). It is in many diverse ventures such as construction; engineering services, education (Madar International School); technology; safety and security; hospitality; health care, auto care; interior design, and oil and gas services. All the ventures were consolidated in 1995. Going with foreign partners in Abu Dhabi or abroad for deals, Bin Salem Holding's diversification makes it a true player as a micro-Vision 2030 itself.

It partnered with world's biggest caviar factory, Germany's United Food Technologies, to establish a farm in Abu Dhabi as a pioneer in aquaculture.[35] The farm-bred sturgeon fish is from Frankfurt as a start, and there are plans to farm the Caspian breeds soon. The venture is considered pro-sustainable environment as some 85% of sturgeon species have been classified rare and face extinction. Because of their long reproductive cycle, long migration, and sensitivity to environmental conditions such species are under severe threat from poaching and water pollution. So farmed sturgeon fish is an answer to such problems.

By-products include high-nutrition water for other agricultural pursuits. They are environmentally-additive and friendly. With German expertise and technology, aquaculture can spin off as an emerging cluster involving biotechnology and other hard sciences. Equally strategic is a home-grown food industry for food security. Abu Dhabi imports over 80% of its food to justify agribusiness as a viable cluster.

Expanding abroad is the Al-Futtaim Group (http://www.futtaim.com) which has acquisitions in Saudi Arabia to complement its

---

[35] Equivalent to 10 football fields, the new 60,000-square metre desert caviar and fish farm costing Dh450 million with funding from shareholders and Abu Dhabi Commercial Bank will produce 32 tonnes of caviar and 700 tonnes of sturgeon meat yearly. The UAE alone needs 35 tonnes with 90% of the world's caviar from the Caspian Sea with traditional producers in Iran, Azerbaijan and Russia now hardly harvesting enough for their own national demand; *The National,* April 7, 2011 and June 8, 2011, *Gulf News* and *Khaleej Times,* June 8, 2011.

existing core business and raise its Saudi profile.[36] The conglomerate is no longer interested in minority stakes or financial investment, preferring 100% acquisition or controlling stake acquisitions of business. Its five core business comprises automotive; retail; financial services; property; and electronics and engineering with automotive as the largest in revenue, dominating the UAE car market, by distributing Toyota, Lexus, Honda, Volvo, Chrysler, Dodge vehicles.

The Al-Futtaim Group's retail operations include Ikea, Plug-Ins and Marks & Spencer brands. It is a relatively small player in the Saudi automotive business where it distributes various brands. It takes time, so they represent small and patient acquisitions. Funded by combined equity and bank loans, Al Futtaim is not considering share flotation or tapping the capital markets at a group level. Bond issuances at individual business levels may be an option in the future.

In sharp contrast is a chastened sale, literally and figuratively, of family jewels as a lesson for Damas Jewellery and a wake-up call for other complacent investors.[37] Its owners (three brothers) are held responsible by regulator Dubai International Financial Centre for withdrawing Damas cash and gold without the approval from the other shareholders. Even after being fined, censured, and resigning from their executive positions, they have not repaid the funds.

The parties involved do not have any comprehensive agreement to restructure the debts. The total obligations as what is owed by the brothers are held up in negotiations. Their creditors are the same as Damas creditors in a complicated web linking three groups: three brothers, Damas and banks. Some of the brothers' borrowings are guaranteed by Damas assets. Since the global financial crisis, restructuring, consolidation and other euphemisms are a reality check to transform all to be competitive and lean.

---

[36] Two acquisitions worth $500 million make a small toehold, but important entry for Al-Futtaim of over 70 years with over 40 companies and 20,000 employees in at least 20 countries as one of the Middle East's most recognisable multinational brands; *The National*, May 22, 2011 and www.futtaim.com.

[37] It is a long drawn affair since 2010 for the three Abdullah brothers as the third generation in a 104-year jewellery institution; *The National*, April 5 and 19, 2011.

A typical victim of nontransparency, the Damas story is a victim of its own success. Weak safeguards and problems existed well before its initial public offer in 2008. The Damas affair has begun to affect ordinary and institutional investors, Dubai's reputation, and the Dubai Financial Services Authority as a regulator. It chronicled the problems in Damas business matters in detail; otherwise shrouded as family affairs.

The above four case-studies are varied: A young Emirati with the gumption to join the innovative spirit that Vision 2030 seeks; the second case highlights the success of an already established family-owned holding company initiating a start-up in a new field; the third is an experienced older family-owned holding group which is also expanding, but along its safe traditional core business lines; and finally, the fourth case exhibits a family-owned business due to lack of corporate governance; the company is impaired, and the brothers cannot rejoin as corporate chiefs.

If starting up small and medium-sized enterprises by the Khalifa Fund is not easy, a harder task is to ensure that such individual or family-owned business are sustained and competitive as a strong socio-economic pillar in Vision 2030. The Union Bank of Switzerland and Hongkong and Shanghai Banking Corporation offer succession planning services. A critical success factor is the educated young in a family.

The biggest domestic challenge is a successful transformation of family business in both senses of generational succession and structural change. The right structure and business model is the driving force encompassing many elements, none of which is easy. One is a strategic rationalisation and consolidation of core competencies to restructure from an accumulated diverse range of holdings. It involves strategic disposal of non-core assets while strengthening the core ones.

Diversification accompanied with financial restructuring are in strategic mergers and acquisitions, divestment, company sale, monetisation in initial public offers, tender offers and such. Corporate governance in a family constitution and family council are mechanisms to maintain and balance cohesion as essential to preserve family permanence and continuity in a transparent and competitive world. Sensitivity and conformance to Islamic banking and insurance principles are value-added elements as pro-family.

Realistically, these are ideal standard corporate critical factors for success. The local business culture needs to know the way to customise systems as comfortably acceptable. In turn, the right business model and formulation in place preserves generational succession, family values and traditional brands with external, legal, fiscal, technical, other corporate governances and rules in unison. This way, no enterprise will be left behind in Vision 2030.

Factors affecting generational succession and alternatives include the state of the industry consolidation, not just individual corporate situations. Issues are not only for the family members, but the treatment of nonfamily professionals in resolving any family disputes and conflict of interests arising in decision-making.

A distinction of what triggers succession that categorises family business is a triage process to deal with occurrences. An immediate crisis is upon the death of a founding father if there is no heir groomed. Transition candidates are for mergers and acquisitions or initial public offers. Monetisation in post-transition has outside investors and owners as private equity investment funds appear in joint management of a family's wealth.

As in a medical triage, family-owned business would sort out those needing emergency attention, those with time to wait and those for follow-up in wealth analysis and projection. Prevention is always better than cure. Banks help in technical asset allocation and risk analysis, selection of managers in investment, portfolio execution, monitoring, wealth protection by risk isolation, capital preservation and more succession planning.

In generational succession, the family business goes through phases from pioneer to growth, strategic positioning, consolidation and succession. Parallel to these growth phases, the family-owned company develops from private equity to private placement, initial public offers and a new capital structure, with regulatory listing incentives. A clear roadmap for family governance structure and the tools in shareholder pooling agreement, voting trust and boards is to secure transition and liquidity mechanisms.

The future agenda includes a focus on expansion and growth. One route takes a family business from the familiar domestic to external business terrain, if so desired and appropriate. Some family business as small and medium-sized enterprises may wish to remain small as a preferred option, dedicated to certain local socio-cultural lines of business as their competitive advantage. Small is still beautiful, without being export-oriented or as multinational corporations located abroad.

Others may wish to be big and outward-bound for economies of scale (lower cost with larger output volumes limited to UAE market size) and economies of scope (lower cost through a diversified, related range of products). Diversity and plurality in a range of family business by size, geography and scope are perfectly acceptable in Vision 2030.

It is neither forgotten nor assumed that all migrants are employees. Banks offer higher limits for loans and pro-business financial packages. Many are self-employed as minority partners with Emiratis in business from big supermarket chains to other small and medium-sized enterprises. Some join Emirati entrepreneurs helped by the Khalifa Fund and others. A new breed of nonlocal entrepreneurs is constructive. Therefore there are positive signs that a new corporate environment and breed of entrepreneurs are evolving as directly or indirectly shaped by Vision 2030.

Without a comprehensive, representative big picture of all small and medium-sized and family-owned enterprises, the story is anecdotal. A sobering, poignant point is to know how ready is the local industrial and business community to partner with Abu Inc in Vision 2030. It takes two hands to clap. A responsive, proactive, and vibrant private sector is one of the key thrust and goal of Vision 2030. Its rightful role as a growth engine that makes an interesting appropriate lead-in to laws and regulations.

4.5. Enabling Laws and Regulations

Both Abu Dhabi Vision 2030 and UAE Vision 2021 for a knowledge-based economy need laws and regulations enforced in commensurate. At the outset, the UAE and Abu Dhabi are not short in laws, but seriously short in enforcement. In a constantly changing living environment nothing is static. It is universal that regulators play catch-up information communication technology induced globalisation; the global financial crisis birthed the US Frank–Dodd Act and Basel III.

It is not facetious to observe that any law made is meant to be broken. Loopholes and legal technicalities in both laws and enforcement are exploited. Financial innovations are cleverly deployed by unregulated greed. Anachronistic, run-out-of-date, acquiescent or weak laws become a deterrent and barrier to harm the credibility of a legal system.

Many federal laws, both proposed and being amended are germane to the story of Abu Dhabi's economic development. The process is arduous and time-consuming. The Federal National Council with half of its members elected is not a law-making parliament in the conventional sense. Its members are not lawmakers or legislators, only strictly in a consultative capacity.[38] They are empowered to summon and question any federal minister regarding performance and budget matters.[39]

A ministry first gets the cabinet's permission to draft a law. It is shared with all concerned in the government and private sector for feedback or be scrubbed. The Ministry of Justice's legal technical committee and host ministry jointly amend the bills before referral to the ministerial legal

---

[38] This is as clarified as 70,000 Emiratis vote in 2011, as nine times more than in 2006 and five times the legal minimum of the number of eligible electors of 12,000. It reflects a push for participation, partly the result of the Arab Spring. The Minister of State for the Federal National Council Affairs noted that universal suffrage rather than appointing electors may not be right for the UAE based on the histories of others. With different perspective of the future, what is good for one country is not necessarily good for the other; *The National*, May 25, 2011.

[39] Federal National Council members criticised many federal ministries and institutions on accounting failures, repeated violations of spending habits and failure to spend allotted budgets to implement projects including the federal housing programme. Only 3,000 of 75,000 applications in 2009 obtained funding from Sheikh Zayed Housing Programme. Inconsistencies with a decentralised approach are shown after budgets are approved as ministries control bank accounts; *Khaleej Times*, December 23, 2009.

committee, then back to cabinet and Federal National Council.[40] It is the last stop for any law before the Ministry of Presidential Affairs issues it.

A committee of the Federal National Council reported a continuation of several financial violations and breaches in federal institutions in 2010. An overhaul of internal auditing and legal accountability is required for the budgetary system. The 2006 federal budget first tried for a balanced budget before a zero-based budget regime for three-years (i.e. 2010–2013). The UAE is the first in the region for such an integrated budget zero-based and performance-based budget system for fiscal discipline.

Annual budgets are part of a three-year budget with flexibility to implement various programmes more transparently. Budget preparation has tighter monitoring of various schemes to maximise social impact. Zero-budgeting over three-year allows a longer timeline for project-based financial allocation to prioritise resources in contrast to annual item-based budgeting.

There is neither clarity nor timetable for the emergence of laws. The most awaited is the 51:49 ownership rule to open competition in some sectors. The relevant laws include UAE Commercial Companies Law Federal Law No. 8 of 1984, amended by Law No. 13 and 15 of 1988. It is based primarily on similar European civil jurisdictions. It does not cover civil companies and service establishments which are under the UAE Civil Transactions Law No. 5 of 1985.[41]

---

[40] Interestingly, a visit to Ministry of Justice in 2007 by the UAE Vice-President finding no electronic archiving system, accordingly had computers installed to improve performance and speed up transactions including court hearings and translating all 681 federal laws into English in the first phase. Arabic remains the official language as clearly enunciated in 2008.

[41] It is worth noting that contracts involving an Abu Dhabi entity are specifically governed by Abu Dhabi laws with UAE laws also applicable. Parties may not realise that invoking Abu Dhabi laws in a contract imports specific provisions relating to interests not applied in a wider UAE context. Specifically, the status of interest paid in the UAE (12%) differs from Abu Dhabi (9%). The UAE's general position allows for interest in commercial dealings in both the Commercial Code and Civil Code. If parties want to agree specific rates of interest, it is best to record accordingly in the contract, as courts are unlikely to award higher of 12%; usury constitutes an offence under the UAE Penal Code.

The distinction between civil and commercial companies is inherited or adopted from Egyptian laws. Civil companies and service establishments involve the exploitation of personal expertise of skills of the proprietor. Non-nationals can open service firms to practice a vocation or profession. Pending amendments or a new investment law, some industries may be liberalised up to 75% or 100% outside free zones.

The sole agency law, which is due for amendment, is gradually opened as by-parallel imports to curb inflationary trends and changes in sponsorship. The original intent for a local sponsor with local knowledge and connections or *wasta* for application of licenses or work permits ensures that the foreigners are abiding by local custom and business practices. The agent gets an arranged fee, not equity participation.

However, the UAE sole agency law has provisions for exclusivity, tantamount to monopoly. Foreign companies cannot have more than one agent in one territory, though they can have different agents for different lines of products. Over time, as an added layer of business cost, it has been abused by both parties. The new amendments ensure greater transparency to settle disputes between principals and agents.

Nationals want to register their sponsorship with the Ministry of Economy as a protection, having invested resources and time as the exclusive agent. As they may do so without informing the principal sponsored, a lack of transparency creates misunderstanding. Changing sponsors by the principal is not simple to render inflexibilities in other ways including workers' visas tied to the sponsors, without mobility to change jobs until changes in 2011.

Theoretically, foreign companies have four ways to distribute their goods and services. One is through 100% owned branches where only a national service agent is appointed without stakes as ownership or profit of the company and can be changed any time as per the agreement by the foreign company.

Two is through subsidiaries subjected to 51% UAE or GCC citizens' participation outside the free zones. Three is through nonexclusive distributors. These agreements cannot be registered in the Ministry of Economy, meant only for exclusive agents' agreements. Finally, contracts are registered if the local agent wishes for protection under UAE laws.

Negotiations of free trade agreements since 2005 have raised concerns for some amendments to the sole agency law. A principal can rescind an agency agreement only upon justification. A commercial agency is not authorised to re-enter the commercial agents' registered by using another agent or sponsor. Its defined term is deemed as terminated upon its expiry unless both parties agree to extend it.

Exceptions to the old rule that goods, products, materials, or other assets for trading cannot be brought in via a channel other than the agent including materials for trading has since been liberalised.[42] The unconditional parallel import of 15 main foodstuffs to fight inflation in 2007–2008 was sanctioned expeditiously, with 15 new items added since 2011.[43]

The UAE bankruptcy or insolvency law was promulgated as early as 1973 and amended under the UAE Federal Commercial Transactions Law No. 18 in 1993. Articles No. 645 to 900 of the 1993 law are clear to cover all aspects of bankruptcy pertaining to merchants and companies. It is similar to international bankruptcy laws by scope and procedures in terms of notice issued to all creditors to register their claims and any subsequent objections to the amounts stated by the courts.

The UAE needs clearer rules to regulate bankruptcy and insolvency of individuals and companies. Individuals in default in personal loans cannot announce bankruptcy as they are under the UAE civil laws. Bankruptcy strictly applies to business and traders covered by the UAE Federal Commercial Transactions Law No. 18 in 1993 and not to civil debtors covered by the UAE Civil Transactions.

Traders defined in both the Commercial Transactions Law and Commercial Companies Law in commercial activities are differentiated

---

[42] The UAE became the first in the Gulf to join the Admission Temporaire/ Temporary Admission or ATA Carnet system to allow nonperishable goods imported temporarily without pay customs duties or taxes for up to a year. Carnet merchandise passports benefit trade shows, fairs and exhibitors and others in tourism, transport and entertainment including concerts and sports events.

[43] Together with disallowing retailers charge additional commission fees on credit card usage on goods, not services, the Supreme Committee for Consumer Protection in the Ministry of Economy liberalised trade of 15 more products from detergents to fats and oil; *The National* and *Gulf News*, June 8, 2011.

from individuals or companies in professional and consultancy activities including, doctors, lawyers, consulting engineers, and others. The distinction is purely arbitrary and hereditary from antiquated Egyptian laws.

More fundamental is with convergence arising from knowledge-based goods-services and manufacturing-services, multi-purpose clustered conglomerates like Japanese *keiretsu* or Korean *chaebol*. A conglomerate would need multiple licenses defined for manufacturing, trading, or finance.[44]

The Commercial Companies Law sets down the exclusions of companies in special agreements with the UAE and local governments encompassing companies in oil and gas and in free zones. Foreign banks comply with all the registration requirements to establish branches, but are exempted from having to appoint sponsors.

In time as UAE laws get up to speed, the delineation of Dubai's free zones to be competitively ahead of rigid UAE laws may be less sharp. They are *ultra vires* as non-UAE territories, subject to various emirates' laws as a trade-off.

In 2009, the law was amended to allow limited liability companies to determine the size of capital, abolishing the minimum capital requirement bank guarantee, resulting in less time and bureaucratic procedures. The prescribed capital was Dh150,000 or $40,000. But Dubai mandates at Dh300,000, which is twice the minimum amount.

The Commercial Companies Law also defines what is deemed as commercial for activities in the Commercial Transaction Law. These include companies dealing in various commodities and services and those under professions including by non-nationals.

The laws are meticulous and laborious in detailed listing of activities together with what the Commercial Transaction Law itself defines traders broadly as covering companies and individuals who carry out

---

[44] Both the Ministry of Economy and Abu Dhabi's Department of Economic Development have separately issued publications of their standard classification of economic activities, both following the UN International Standard Industrial Classification.

commercial activities. As working procedures, nothing seems to have fallen through the crevices with two laws in operation.

Failure of companies and individuals to apply for declaration of bankruptcy makes them liable to criminal prosecution under the UAE Penal Code, Federal Law 3 of 1987. Local business customs do prevail, as for non-traders with their debts exceeding liabilities or creditors who use a process known as *hajr* in Arabic for restrictions with some similarities to bankruptcy.

Proper dealing involves all the authorities including the Ministry of Economy, various chambers of commerce and industry, licensing authorities, and the Central Bank. Closing up a business or dealing with bankruptcy can be as much a hassle as in any emerging economy. Therefore, the uncharted territory comprises traditional and cultural legislative norms that catch up with, or transcends a knowledge-based business model.

A federal Consumer Protection Law No. 24 of 2006 has established a Supreme Committee for Consumer Protection and a Consumer Protection Department as two bodies to administer consumer rights. The Ministry of Economy is empowered to monitor price changes to control inflation, promote fair competition, and eradicate monopolies.

Abu Dhabi's Department of Economic Development has its own regulations on consumer protection related to its business licensing mandate. It acts on consumer complaints with obligations imposed on suppliers on advertisements, labels, spare parts, and warranties. Its Quality Control Council on all aspects of health, environment, and safety works with the federal Emirates Standardisation and Metrology Authority.

Separately, the Ministry of Justice contemplates a new federal draft law to streamline, codify, and unify all the doctrinal provisions, penalties, and blood money. The new Personal Status Law with 196 articles is enforced to find a way out for the different and inconsistent verdicts issued. Judges quote from and rely on opinions of the jurisprudence schools. A new all-inclusive federal law would leave no room for discretionary or interpretative judgement.

The Electronics Transactions Law No. 1 of 2006 which regulates and applies to electronic records, documents, and signatures connected with electronic transactions and e-commerce does not include matters on personal law for marriage, divorce, wills and deeds of title for immovable property. Its main objective is to minimise forgery as e-commerce and e-transactions grow. There is no taxation on e-commerce. The Ministry of Foreign Trade issues Arabic Certificates of Origin online as e-government.

A separate Law on Combating Cyber Crimes No. 2 of 2006 superseded any conflicting previous or local laws. The definitions are broadly drafted to cover all aspects of information technology crimes. The law is a penal code and activation of its legal positions does not need an official compliant or a plaintiff for public prosecution which can act solely against any violation of this law.

Law No. 2 of 2006 has 29 articles to combat cyber crime. Article 2 is on any intentional act resulting in destroying or revealing secrets or republishing personal or official information as a crime as in logging into an information website or system. It is comprehensive in covering all forms of cyber offences and even protects family principles, values and private life of family members.

There is yet to be a full-bodied law on intellectual property rights to combat the trade in fake or counterfeit products and other fraudulent activities. *Ad hoc* changes in federal laws include the amended Law No. 7 for 2002 on copyrights and related rights and a federal law No. 17 for 2002 on industrial patent rights, designs, and industrial patterns. It abrogated Federal Law No. 44 and was amended in 2006.

Laws on the environment make another new area. The UAE has one of the world's biggest in carbon footprint in consumption of energy per capita. Anti-pollution laws will enable financial and environment gains as in greater use of natural gas, especially for vehicles. The green building codes by the Abu Dhabi Municipality is in motion with delays in classification and other technical and administrative hurdles.

With the global financial crisis, international arbitration has gained some traction and pace. Arbitration can occur locally at the Abu Dhabi Chamber of Commerce and Industry, Dubai International

Arbitration Centre or Dubai International Financial Centre — London Court of International Arbitration. A choice of forum in regional and international arbitration centres and courts include the United Nations Commission on International Trade Law.[45]

At the local level in Abu Dhabi, the Department of Economic Development has completed its comprehensive review of all economic laws and international trade conventions with an aim to identify areas for legal amendments, new laws and regulations to improve the business environment.[46] A consultative paper is being prepared to include appropriate solutions by consultations, coordination, including a questionnaire to relevant sectors and 25 government entities.

At a later phase of the project, comprehensive benchmarks for proposed amendments will follow with workshops on best practices. It would conclude with final recommendations for decision-makers in 2012. The proposed field survey covers some 283 private firms and institutions in Abu Dhabi, representing the business, industrial and tourism sectors with diverse nationalities.

4.6. Trade Policy and WTO

Abu Dhabi's industrialisation is hinged on direct exports rather than *entrepôt* trade and knowledge-based services. It has to pay attention to, and exert its influence to know the way the Ministry of Foreign Trade mediates its trade policy and investment policy. Since its first WTO trade policy review in 2006, it did an exemplary, voluntary review in 2010 (UAE Ministry of Foreign Trade, 2010).

In particular, the UAE's commitments and obligations to the WTO and free trade agreements[47] need expertise in international

---

[45] Given the complexity, the United Nations Commission on International Trade Law (UNICITRAL) was developed in 1976 a special set of arbitration rules. These rules have been widely used all over the world and can be referred to by the parties.
[46] No details are revealed of what laws are reviewed, a work-in-progress; *The National*, March 27, 2011.
[47] Following the GCC charter's Article 31, all UAE bilateral free trade agreements become GCC free trade agreements. GCC free trade agreements in negotiation

trade and international laws. One set of concerns is the classification of oil and gas trade as commodity or energy services and their respective regulations.

Various country papers by the US, Canada, Norway, EU, Chile, and Venezuela are submitted to the WTO. The US in its initial negotiations for a free trade agreement has emphasised energy services as under GATS.

A strategic trade policy for the UAE including Abu Dhabi is sensitive to the political economy of trade as international economics and international relations. With geoeconomics and geopolitics, trade is inherently nuanced in a globalised mental mode. Vision 2030 for export-oriented industrialisation and economic transformation has heed thinking and policy-setting both in the UAE and externally at the GCC or WTO.

A foreign economic policy rather than the traditional bifurcation into economic and foreign affairs is preferred for Abu Dhabi in two ways. One is a foreign economic policy including cooperation and economic agreement in the first instance, as more pragmatic and realistic. Therefore, political economy trade issues blur the distinction between political regionalism and economic regionalisation.

Two is effective and timely implementation of Abu Dhabi's strategic foreign economic policy in its proposed export and investment promotion agencies geared to competitive domestic exports can be exemplary for the UAE. It is unlike Dubai's import-substitution industrialisation and *entrepôt* trade. Dubai is a trading hub rests on managing its world-class infrastructure so efficiently that others cannot bypass by more direct trade.

Much was learnt from negotiating free trade agreements with the US and Australia. The UAE started with the big, rather than the smaller nations to learn and gain confidence, well enough to lead

include the EU, China, Turkey, Pakistan, India, European Free Trade Area, Japan, Mercosur, Australia, New Zealand, Korea, Canada and Malaysia; see the inaugural newsletter, "Trade Affairs" by UAE Ministry of Foreign Trade, Issue 1, March 2009, http://www.moft.gov.ae. The first was signed with Singapore in 2008.

and navigate the GCC in the tricky political economy of free trade agreements. Non-trade issues as in the environment and currency wars have turned into North–South power shift issues since the global financial crisis.

The most relevant and needed law is a competition law for free trade. A federal draft was made since 2006, but has not yet materialised the hardest law in market reform. The focus on competition is only for consumer protection[48] in price and quality to eliminate counterfeits.

A comprehensive competition law is to promote efficiency via competition-based economic reform and effective enforcement. It has a legal mapping to ensure consistency and integrity in sectoral regulations and privatisation policies in two main policy areas. A typical format eschews price fixing and other cartel arrangements; abuses of a dominant position or monopoly. Antitrust controls collusion and other anti-competitive behaviour.

Dominant position of market power refers to a situation where an enterprise is in a position to control the relevant market to produce, supply, or distribute goods or provision of services. Relevant markets for sellers and buyers exchange goods that require delineation by product and geography to include all substitutes and any circumstance realised abroad which affects the domestic market, not circumstances which affect foreign markets.

Restrictive agreements or arrangements such as formal, informal, written or unwritten business practices are acts or behaviour which limit access to markets or unduly restrain competition. A merger and acquisition referring to two or more enterprises legally unify ownership of assets and shares can lead to less competition.

Some listing of restrictive trading agreements or arrangements is illustrative, not exhaustive; Austria lists types of cartels. Anti-competitive agreements and practices between rival or potentially rival firms, regardless of whether such arrangements are written or oral, formal or informal can appreciably prevent, restrict, or distort competition.

---

[48] Clyde & Company drafted an Abu Dhabi consumer protection law in 2005 which remained untouched, superceded by federal Emirates Standardisation and Metrology Authority.

They comprise horizontal price agreements for cartels, informal collusion for price fixing or other terms of sale; bid-rigging, collusive tendering behavior; sharing markets or customer allocation to keep out competition; limit or control production, sale including by quota and investment, concerted refusals to purchase or supply; and collective denial of access to an arrangement or association.

Circumstantial on a case-by-case approach includes fixing trading conditions; joint purchasing and selling; sharing business information (trade secrets to be decided); exchanging price and nonprice information; restricting advertising; getting technical or design standards; refusal to supply an existing customer; and predatory pricing price discrimination as cross subsidisation.

Less apparent are mergers to competition as control by mergers and acquisitions and joint ventures, vertical agreements between suppliers and distributors to foreclose markets to new competitors. These involve companies with a defined amount of turnover may lead to market power. The UAE may be along the anti-trust path, but still far from mergers and acquisitions in vertical agreements.

A rule-of-reason approach applies for selected mergers and acquisitions if there are efficiencies or other offsetting benefits or public interest. Activities which contribute to improving the production or distribution or to promoting technical or economic progress, allow consumers a fair share of the resulting benefit that are thus allowed versus abuse of dominant position.

Included are takeovers, concentrative joint ventures, other acquisitions of control such as interlocking directorates and horizontal merger where the two merging companies produce similar product in the same industry, not vertical mergers where firms are at different production stages of the same good.

It would be particularly tricky for Abu Dhabi Inc and the UAE with many state-owned companies in meeting with direct and indirect state aid to companies as anti-competitive. This is already reflected in charges for the UAE airlines (Chapter 3). The Competition Commission of Singapore and its competition law may be a template.

Special sector and collective interests by sectoral nature cover specific industries in energy, utilities including water, electricity, piped gas, telecommunication, postal services, airlines, cargo terminal operations, railway and road public transport, state-owned enterprises and technology.

Sector-specific is *ex ante* as regulation set in advance versus a competition law as *ex post* regulation as taking action when competition is violated. The non-sectoral, cover certain functions by type of economic arrangements such as specialisation and rationalisation agreements and development of product standards.

Irrespective of their nature and relation to the market, some service activities performed by private or government-owned firms are considered by the government to be of general interest. The providers of services of general interest can be subject to specific obligations such as guaranteeing universal access to various types of quality services at affordable prices. These obligations, covering socio-economic regulations, are set out in transparently.

Any appreciable effect on competition may be guided by a competition test as in indicative market share thresholds comprising agreements made by competing enterprises. Their aggregate market share should not exceed a certain percentage, say 20% in any relevant market.[49]

For non-competing enterprises, their aggregate market share do not exceed 25% in any relevant market. An alternative is to specify thresholds by value. These criteria may define an abuse or acquisition and abuse of a dominant position market power. For mergers and acquisitions, they result in, or are expected to result in a substantial reduction of competition or prevent competition.

A reference is to a person in a business acquisition that includes two or more persons who are interconnected or associated if that person is able to directly or indirectly influence substantially over the activities of the other; those persons in competition in the same market; or one of them supplies to the other.

---

[49] It is 30–40% in industrial economies; top four-firm with 40% market share, three-firm concentrated market with 70% of market, the Herfindahl–Hirschman Index as a sum of squares of the market shares of each firm in the industry. These criteria used by the US Justice Department in anti-trust cases, may be guides.

A competition law provides procedures for notification of mergers and acquisitions and investigation procedures by the competition authority either for confidential guidance as a view of whether activity or behaviour is anti-competitive or a decision whether it is an infringement. The public may make complaints in prescribed forms with the requisite information and documentation to the competition authority of anti-competitive activities or behaviour covered by the scope of the act.

The competition authority like the Telecommunications Regulatory Authority arbitrates and enforces competition. The modalities vary. One is a sector regulator with some or all competition law enforcement functions. Another is the competition authority and sector regulator enforce the competition law in coordination. An advocacy role of the competition authority with regard to regulation and regulatory reform would stress the economic criterion for advocacy. The middle-ground of coordination may be preferred.

On cross-sectoral competition cases or involving cross-cutting issues, the competition authority works with the relevant sectoral regulator. They decide which regulator is best placed to handle the case or issue within the legal ambit of each regulator. The competition authority will work closely with all parties to prevent any double jeopardy and minimise the regulatory burden.

The term "regulation" in the competition law refers to the various instruments by which the government imposes requirements on enterprises and citizens. It thus embraces laws, formal and informal orders, administrative guidance and subordinate rules issued by all levels of government. It also covers rules issued by non-governmental or professional self-regulatory bodies to which the government has delegated regulatory powers.

Regulatory barriers to competition are differentiated from structural and strategic barriers to entry. They result from acts issued or performed by government executive authorities, by local self-government bodies and by non-government or self-regulatory bodies to which the government has delegated regulatory powers. They include administrative barriers to entry into a market, exclusive rights, certificates, licences and other permits for starting business operations.

Sanctions are to be appropriately set, but should emphasise the use of more carrots than sticks with restitution to injured consumers. Appeals will be set. A leniency programme in incentives as in lesser penalties or full immunity from financial penalties may encourage "whistle-blowing" as cartels are hard to detect.

The first party to give evidence of cartel activity is granted full immunity from financial penalty under conditions for full and complete cooperation in Singapore, even when investigation has commenced. Subsequent leniency applications which are not first in line may be granted a reduction of upto 50% in financial penalty. A "whistle-blower" is protected and encouraged to promote self-regulation, prevention-better-than-cure as more efficient and cost-effective.

The UAE has a gradualist approach to a competition law. With convergence and new technologies, regulators tend to be behind the curve of producers and operators. A balance of government-knows-best to be interventionist and private-sector-knows-more for sectoral micro-regulation is premised on social profit versus social profit for government intervention is with a human face for the greater good.

To conclude, foreign firms, direct foreign investment, and big foreign banks are invited for competition to lock-in reform, raise core competencies in various industries so that economic development moves at a faster pace. This is the additional role for a genuine UAE competition law, without compromising emiratisation. Therefore, a political choice remains to pace and juggle a model for the UAE's competition law as Vision 2030 draws near.

Chapter 5

ABU DHABI'S ECONOMIC DEVELOPMENT MODEL

5.1. Introduction

Economic development is defined as the mobilisation of land (natural resources), labour (foreign exceeds local), and capital (oil-wealth). Despite underdeveloped statistics and years of paralysis of analysis, Vision 2030 was prepared in 2008 following the policy agenda and strategic plan of government restructuring in 2007. Vision 2030 represents the aspirations in years of relative boom *vis-à-vis* its rolling-out capability since the global financial crisis of 2008.

Abu Dhabi as a whole sat together as one team for the first time, committed to developing the Vision 2030 document based on a unique set of methodologies, assumptions, and key performance indicators. Vision 2030 was a wish-list even before the global financial crisis of 2008 or the Arab Spring since 2011. Decision-makers remained undaunted, though more sobered since the turn of these events.

The execution of the Vision faces other challenges, one of them being — how to deal with Abu Dhabi's silo-based tribalism. Such challenges are neither surprising nor fatal and the government is confident of deriving the support from all its people to implement Vision 2030. The economics and technical know-how pertaining to Vision 2030, which is a massive and a complex exercise, are new to most of Abu Dhabi across-the-board. In theory, key concepts and processes in layman's terms will need to be communicated to the public to educate them and enhance awareness. Buy-in is a two-way process to consult and give feedback to over 60–70 stakeholders in the public and private sectors. In practice, planning by Abu Dhabi Inc is top-down and consultant-driven.

In order to achieve Vision 2030, Abu Dhabi should initiate efforts to effectively market the concept and nurture the development of a knowledge-based economy. Currently, the private sector alone is designated as a growth engine.

The population and labour force comprising 80% foreigners/migrants worry about job security. The remaining 20% are Emiratis who are secure in all ways, except being a minority in their homeland. This appears to be a recipe for hiccups, not necessarily a failure. Abu Dhabi is doubly blessed by resources and leadership. Orchestrating Vision 2030 requires greater effort in a strategic, pragmatic model.

This chapter first summarises the main findings. Vision 2030 in the right direction so far is more qualitatively anecdotal than by hard performance indicators. Statistics and surveys are considered as works-in-progress. Scenario analysis as part of the planning discipline to recheck assumptions and boundaries requires hard rethinking and work. The world changes constantly.

The proposed new Abu Dhabi model as per the Vision 2030 is analysed comparatively with other benchmark models. Four policy implications of its economic development model as branded are identified and left to the readers to decide; what next and how? Staying on course is imperative for Abu Dhabi's credibility and reputation in managing its political economy of success.

5.2. Main Findings

Abu Dhabi's knowledge-based economy (Fig. 1.1) has an innovation-driven stage added to Porter's factor-, infrastructure-, and wealth-driven model. It attained its rags-to-riches wealth-driven story by its natural comparative advantage in hydrocarbon. More than oil wealth monetised in infrastructure, Abu Dhabi needs a national innovation policy to drive its investments toward innovation and induce competitive advantage.

Of the five options in the UNDP Abu Dhabi Strategic Development Programme, 2000–2020 (Table 1.2), combining the two options for productivity improvement and sectoral restructuring, was the UN's recommendation. These are revisited in Vision 2030, but are oriented more toward diversifying sectors of growth than in productivity growth. A passive reliance on migrant workers has resulted in high quantity of low quality labour without higher productivity.

In a dualistic economy, higher productivity by value-added (Chapter 2) is desired. Productivity growth and improvement need a switch from traditional low-skilled, labour-intensive industries to high skill-intensive, knowledge services and manufacturing. Services delivered via e-commerce and e-government by business process reengineering yields higher productivity with appropriate human resources development.

In 2010, the Dubai General-Secretariat of Executive Council launched its Dubai Model for Government Service Delivery Initiative. Its first phase for best practice and knowledge for service improvement has the Dubai Model Initiative and Services Improvement Government Network focussing on innovation and maximising value through assessment.[1] Abu Dhabi needs a similar model.

Zayed Vision remains evergreen — sustainable economic and ecological development. Traditional hydrocarbon and renewable energy in a green, sustainable ecosystem would support water and food security. What is patently clear is that Vision 2030's diversification continues to be hydrocarbon-finessed. Equally logical is Abu Dhabi staying as an energy capital by going nuclear, literally and figuratively in boldness.

A review of the industrialisation as planned and practised shows many pieces of the jigsaw puzzle (Figs. 2.1, 2.2, 2.3, and 2.4) put in place. Industrialisation, fast-forwarded in five free zones, is in contrast to some 30 in Dubai. Abu Dhabi should not remain a laggard just because it has the oil wealth to industrialise at its own pace. Vision 2030 can be considered as both dare-to-dream and cautious; for example, the recent plan to create a semiconductor hub in Abu Dhabi is a strategic opportunity seized.

Mega projects by Zonescorp, Abu Dhabi Basic Industries Corporation, and Kizad are in Emirates Steel Industries, Emirates

---

[1] *Gulf News*, June 6, 2011.

Aluminium Industries, and downstream plants. Privatisation commercialises some government assets, injects more capital via initial public offers, so that the operators in strategic public–private partnerships get more support. These modalities are pioneered by the Abu Dhabi Water and Electricity Authority and General Holding Company.

Down the industrial hierarchy, the bulked-up Khalifa Fund holding an impressive capital of Dh2 billion, provides funding support to small and medium-sized enterprises including family-owned firms in the region thereby empowers emiratisation, national identity, and young entrepreneurs, as per Porter's five-forces (Fig. 1.2). However, it has stopped short of reiterating productivity for profitability and competitiveness. It truly needs to groom local enterprises, including small and medium-sized ones as supporting industries, with service providers as part of the supply chain development, with room to be multinational corporations, if possible. Vision 2030 needs such support in industries in manufacturing and creative technology-based services, not mere retail and franchises.

A three-in-one case-study of the UAE Offsets Group, Mubadala Development Company, and Advanced Technology Investment Company in Globalfoundries proves Abu Dhabi Inc's prowess to be opportunistic from aerospace to semiconductors. Catalytic sovereign wealth funds in mega projects could embrace in their credo, lean management,[2] productivity and frugal innovations as part of the technology diffusion.

To consolidate and reinforce sustainable industrialisation and economic development, the Technology Development Committee has formulated a science, technology, and innovation policy in coordination with the Abu Dhabi Education Council. Mathematics and science are central in an education-cum-manpower plan. It is hoped that such a move will strengthen the human resources development efforts which until now has been the weakest link.

---

[2]Started by Toyota as lean manufacturing or simply lean as in lean enterprise or lean production centres on preserving value with less work as a practice, weighing expenditure of resources for any goal other with the creation of value for the end customer not to be wasteful. From the perspective of customer, value is defined as any action or process that a customer would be willing to pay for. Governments may not have a profit bottomline, but being lean is about productivity and value for citizens and stakeholders.

Ambitious targets include gross research and development expenditure as a ratio of GDP and research scientists and engineers per 1,000 population. Neither the basis for the bold projections nor actions are clear. In reality, technonationalism prevails over technoglobalism. Multinational corporations retain frontier research and technologies at home for greater synergies and security. It is risky to conduct pure research in countries where the intellectual property rights are inadequate. Only product development occurs as customisation.

Singapore's joint government-business training centres and local industrial upgrading-cum-buddy schemes enhance technology transfers. Several multinational corporations help local partners and suppliers by outsourcing and supply chains to assure skills for quality. Hands-on transfer of technologies, knowledge, and management are tangible and convincing outcomes.

The belief that domestic investment and local enterprises have been alienated *vis-à-vis* direct foreign investment, is misplaced. Such a misunderstanding cannot be corrected by mere dialogues. Merits, such as economies of scale and scope through partnerships to reach external markets are well-proven by East Asian local enterprises including small and medium-sized enterprises. Some of these local enterprises have leapfrogged to become multinational corporations in their own right.

Success stories are required to spur the stagnating manufacturing's contribution to GDP at 7.5% in 2005 and 7.4 % in 2009 (Table 2.1) to 25% as proclaimed in Vision 2030. Forging strategic partnership and alliances are a positive, not a zero-sum game in the globalised competitive marketplace. Learning organisations from state-owned national champions to conservative local firms, growing horizontally and vertically across the supply chain, would leverage up or bridge the gap.

For knowledge-based services, the dominance of real estate in the GDP (Table 2.1) is neither healthy nor sustainable. Financial services, telecommunication, transportation and tourism with information communication technology fit and meet Vision 2030's knowledge-based targets much better. These services would also be able to render high-skilled, professional jobs for Emiratis.

Some cultural obstacles are noted, but they are not insurmountable. The sheer necessity to venture into the private sector via opportunities in services is clear, as already proved by the Etihad Airlines and Emirates Airlines that are globally competitive today. Both national carriers are vanguard to tourism and hospitality services. In time, Abu Dhabi's metro and Etihad Railway linking the UAE to GCC and onward portend more logistics services.

Capital and financial market deepening must accompany long-term financial sector development. Vision 2030 projects will require long-term financing in bonds or *sukuk* and could tap the advantages of Islamic finance. The forces of integration and consolidation of other segments, from banks to equity and stock markets may be trickier. Skills in crisis management[3] are missing amid global financial trend and development.

The follies of rogue banks in irrational exuberance have been identified as the common denominator in several banking and financial crises. They escalate into economic, socio-political crisis as empirically evidenced in the Asian financial crisis. As Winston Churchill had admitted, he could not see his way confidently to any other alternative, but still he "would rather see finance less proud and industry more content" (Best, 2006, p. 119). Vision 2030 has brick-and-mortar downstream industrialisation-cum-services.

Wealth accumulation is not merely in physical assets at home or acquisitions abroad. It cannot be stressed enough that technology acquisition is the base of future wealth beyond hydrocarbon. Human capital or human resources development are part of the equation, as passionately forged as environmental protection by Zayed Vision as a forerunner of Vision 2030. Human survival and quality of life are intrinsically tied to a sustainable eco-system. Ecology in harmony remains natural and wholly sensible.

Human resources development is a two-fold challenge. One is pre-employment education in contrast to post-employment continuous education and training to upgrade skills with ever changing technology. On the other hand, population is destiny. A population

---

[3]Crisis management entails from identifying to responding to turning points in business cycles without much legislative or administrative lags with the right policy tools that inevitably involves trade-off.

policy is ultimately a political decision. A subtle balance of an unimpeded free flow of migrant labour with emiratisation and national identity urges a revisit to an immigration policy for global talent and higher productivity.

As local universities including Masdar Institute revved up, concerted graduate placements become critical to fulfil targets of the Technology Development Committee's Science, Technology and Innovation Policy. Predominantly foreign, the graduates thus recruited are value-added resources, and not mere beneficiaries of scholarships. By the same token, a potential could be the admission of the second-generation children of migrant labour into tertiary colleges.

More than alarming statistics in costs or benefits of foreign labour (Tables 4.1 and 4.2), upgrading to a global talent policy is long past due. Who to retain and retrain, who pays for training and who to wean off as low-skilled, low value-added forms a political economy choice that is aligned to Vision 2030. A pure humanitarian immigration policy to be substituted by economism as a *raison d'etre* is justifiable for Emiratis and their identity.

Labour and employment policies for Emiratis and foreign workers have their own issues and challenges. High voluntary unemployment for Emiratis is neither new nor due to foreigners occupying jobs which Emiratis might want. Cultural dispositions and work attitudes would need to be innovatively altered. A sequestered wealth of human capital is waiting to be unlocked in a higher female labour force participation rate.

It bears repeating and is important to mention here that productivity, both as a concept and practice, is somewhat missing from this equation. This is indeed a blind spot which should be rectified, but needs hard discipline via lean management.

There is no shortage of funds and institutions for human resources development, emiratisation, or small and medium-sized enterprises. From the federal Tanmia since 2002 to the more direct Abu Dhabi Tawteen Council, UAE Academy or Khalifa Fund — they all require a shift from quota to qualitative emiratisation. An education-cum-manpower plan is required, which may consume time and statistics, even beyond 2030, but is worthwhile are needed.

Four case-studies comprising three successful local business models and one failure model are anecdotal rather than any generalised empirical evidence. Visionary local firms are partners to Abu Dhabi Inc thereby generating several micro-visions matching the goal of Vision 2030. One entrepreneur in his start-up has a dare-to-dream attitude harnessing his idealism to incorporate new technologies including crowd-sourcing in a doll.

Two other successful cases of family-owned conglomerates are contrasted. One is a change agent-cum-game changer pioneering in aquaculture with German expertise in a local farm-based caviar and fish. Another enterprise focuses on its core competencies to expand into Saudi Arabia. All successful cases and when multiplied across-the-board would ensure Vision 2030 with a new breed of private sector-led entrepreneurs in new or existing fields.

The failed case offers lessons in corporate governance in accountability and transparency to be grafted onto traditional family-owned business. These are not necessarily inferior in management or technology. The right corporate leadership to mimic and replicate a myriad of micro-visions are the basic building blocks to Vision 2030.

Dubai World's hardships and punctuated speculative real estate bubble offer the same lesson. Corporate social responsibility, corporate governance, transparency and accountability form a tied package. Off-plan sales in real estate, when better regulated in parallel with more viable financial products, benefit both buyers and sellers.

An environment conducive to business, investment and technology transfer needs the right set of laws and regulations. There is no shortage of laws and regulations which are mainly borrowed from Egypt. Many of these laws require improvisations to suit the demands of the 21st century. The legal environment for Vision 2030 also needs an efficient and effective enforcement which is presently lacking.

To take-off into the globalised 21st century of economic development, a laborious time-consuming and difficult process of amending and modifying laws and introducing new ones should be undertaken. Abu Dhabi as the largest emirate holds some sway to affect international legal agreements in trade and investment befitting Vision 2030.

Abu Dhabi as a free trader in multilateral WTO trade liberalisation graduates into bilateral free trade agreements with GCC and other regional pacts like Arab League. It gains economic and legal skills working with the Ministry of Foreign Trade in a strategic, competitive trade policy to open markets. A developed country status is not by per capita GDP alone. In order to be a contributing global player, Abu Dhabi must manage its pace well in qualitative terms.

A competition law is much more than dealing with protection of consumer rights against inflation or pirated counterfeits. It is the hardest, but most needed law for a small, open Abu Dhabi in export-oriented industrialisation reliant on reciprocal free trade. An opportunity exists for antitrust law and institution to lock-in domestic reforms for competition.

A snapshot of achievements shows some outcomes as opportunistic beside those planned in Vision 2030. These are credited to change agents in autonomous agencies including the Mubadala Development Company and its associates from the Masdar Initiative to the Advanced Technology Investment Company, especially in Globalfoundries. Curiously, this set of DNA is not easily found in the wider bureaucracy of Abu Dhabi.

Bureaucrats as change agents struggle to garner momentum down the line to implement consultancy plans. Economic and technical details are daunting. Although foreign experts have the requisite domain knowledge, they do not possess local knowledge and experiences. These are often complicated by non-transparency and nuanced political economy. Project management offices, in-house training and development units or other micro-offices create more silos or tasks to be endlessly coordinated.

Vision 2030 is crafted without a singular overarching economic development agency and, until latterly, a whole-of-government culture. The Executive Council started with over 60 entities and stakeholders in the government machinery to coordinate and align for Vision 2030. The Department of Economic Development has over 75 partners in working out its economic development plan.

Tribal capitalism as a DNA can be both unifying and divisive. It is complicated by multicultural diversity of 80% expatriates jointly implementing Vision 2030. Knitting micro-visions together proved more time- and energy-consuming, but not impossible with political will and commitment. Profit-motivated micro-corporate in parallel with Vision 2030 would be expeditious, faster, and game-changing.

5.3. Vision 2030 Benchmarking

Norway as an advanced oil and OECD industrial economy is an obvious comparator. In real 2005 terms, Norway's GDP per capita at $64,000 was second, ranked among 181 countries, Abu Dhabi came third at $55,600 GDP per capita and the UAE at $27,000 finsihed at 23rd position. In the UNDP human development index in 2004 for 178 countries, their respective scores were Norway at top at 0.97, 30th at 0.89 by Abu Dhabi's own study and the UAE at 0.84 as 50th.

Other comparators include Ireland, Canada, US, UK, and Singapore. Beside the Group of Seven (G7), others admired for reform and private sector-led transformation include South Korea (Pirie, 2008), Hong Kong, Sweden, Finland, and New Zealand. Others are referred by consultants for specifics as in health and education. The learning curve is steep and time-consuming. Whither 2030 as a hard or soft target is a *double-entendre*?

Abu Dhabi's GDP per capita in 2009 was $90,402 (Dh332,500). The UAE's the human development index at 0.82 was ranked 32nd in 2010. Despite the slight fall from 0.84 in 2005, the UAE was ahead of Qatar and Bahrain ranked 38th and 39th, respectively. The UAE is 23rd in 2010 in the Global Competitiveness Index and 33rd in World Bank's Doing Business Survey. New Zealand is top in Transparency International's Corruption Perception Index in 2010. The UAE is 30th globally and 2nd regionally.

Beside the federal Emirates National Competitiveness Council since 2008, the Competitive Office of Abu Dhabi in the Department of Economic Development is tasked in 2011 to create a sustainable environment that would enable firms and people to realise their full productive potential at both the micro- and macro-levels. It seeks the right policies in conjunction with a cluster mapping of stakeholders/sectors that also feature in Vision 2030.

Table 5.1 puts together identified sectors in Vision 2030 and Department of Economic Development's various plans. Until more

Table 5.1. Sectors under Vision 2030 and Development of Economic Development.

Vision 2030 done in 2008	Department of Economic Development		Competitive office of Abu Dhabi 2011 (same as Vision 2030)
	Economic development strategic plan for 2008–2012	Industrial strategy 2011 (only manufacturing)	
(1) Energy (other than oil and gas)	(1) Energy (other than oil and gas)	(1) Aerospace	(1) Energy (other than oil and gas)
(2) Petrochemicals	(2) Petrochemicals	(2) Construction materials	(2) Petrochemicals
(3) Metals and mining	(3) Building materials	(3) Engineered metal products	(3) Metals
(4) Aviation, aerospace and defence	(4) Civil aviation	(4) Food processing	(4) Aviation, aerospace and defence
(5) Pharmaceuticals, biotechnology and life sciences	(5) Renewable energy	(5) Oilfield equipment	(5) Pharmaceuticals, biotechnology and life sciences
(6) Tourism	(6) Tourism	(6) Packaging	(6) Tourism
(7) Healthcare equipment and services	(7) Transport and logistics	(7) Plastics	(7) Healthcare equipment and services
(8) Transportation, trade and logistics	(8) Media	(8) Renewable technologies	(8) Transportation, trade and logistics
(9) Education	(9) Financial services	(9) Transportation equipment	(9) Education
(10) Media	(10) Information communication technology	(10) Semiconductor (1–9 are based on existing anchors of petrochemicals, steel and aluminium)	(10) Media
(11) Financial services			(11) Financial services
(12) Telecommunication services			(12) Telecommunication services

Source: Drawn by author from http//www.abudhabi.ae, http//www.adeconomy.ae and press releases. Sectors in the Technology Development Committee's Science, Technology and Innovation Policy remain a works-in-progress, but likely to synchronise to those already identified above.

statistics are available to show how industrial restructuring and diversification are progressing, 10–12 sectors as variously identified encompass a non-oil knowledge-based economy. The journey in learning and exposure for the private sector to join Abu Dhabi Inc is more important than the destination. The final list of sectors adjusts, morphs, and changes continuously to a core as more action-ready.

Comparing restructuring and diversification in Abu Dhabi with other country models from oil to non-oil cannot be sector by sector. Sectors arise from comparative and competitive advantages. Norway has more fishery resources and capabilities. Singapore has no oil, but it is the world's third largest refinery with downstream petrochemicals and specialty chemicals, upstream oil exploration, and other oil trading services.

The criteria for industrialisation and diversification hold for a knowledge-based economy. Knowledge-intensive manufacturing and service clusters in research and development include testing or clinical trials, warehousing and storage and the full range of telecommunication, logistics, and information communication technology. The degree and pace of advancement along the value chain depend on human resources capabilities.

Singapore's model of economic development under the Ministry of Trade and Industry has a family of statutory boards. The Economic Development Board leads industrialisation (Low *et al.*, 1993; Schein, 1996; and Koh, ed, 2002), focused on foreign investment. By 1968, it spun off Jurong Town Corporation in industrial estates and the Development Bank of Singapore for industrial financing.

Likewise, in Abu Dhabi, the Department of Economic Development at the state-level equivalent of a ministry has Zonescorp which is like the Jurong Town Corporation. Instead of a national agency for industrial finance, many national champions in oil and gas, sovereign wealth funds and the rest of Abu Dhabi Inc have financed mega-projects. They are the catalysts for banks to go downstream to finance other private sector projects for Vision 2030.

As much as government-knows-best in Abu Dhabi Inc's tribal capitalism or Singapore Inc's paternalistic nanny state (Low *et al.*, 2001), the private sector knows-more in the new knowledge-based economy. Sectors and activities better suited as *laissez-faire* to tap the direct foreign investment and multinational corporations are balanced by state capitalism for social or public goods with externalities.

Key performance indicators do more than track, monitor, or measure programmes. They are benchmarks to match and upgrade to global standards, quality and best practices as statistics and comparators to provide a macro-picture to show further directions for policy and actions. Alignments or adjustments make them Abu Dhabi-centric indicators. Abu Dhabi must first upgrade its third-world statistics to match its first-world wealth.

5.4. Scenarios

Policy-makers are increasingly presented with more than a scenario as definitive interpretation. A single outcome typically understates uncertainty (impossible probability) and risk (relatively tractable aspect of uncertainty). Familiar risk notions have deeper layers or predicaments of ambiguity and ignorance as noted by Knight (1921) or Kuhn's paradigm shifts (1962 and 1996).

Risk arises when individuals or groups are confident in accumulated knowledge or experience. Risk-taking by the definitive entrepreneur is as good as Schumpeterian's concept of "creative destruction". In an uncertainty, confidence is in the knowledge of possible outcomes, but not their likelihood owing either to difficulties in prediction or lack of information. A scientific approach faces strong temptations and pressures to treat uncertainty as risk.

Two more problematic aspects of uncertainty arise. One aspect is where being unsure is not just how likely different outcomes are, but also which of these outcomes would be relevant. There is no guarantee under ambiguity, even when the best scientific analysis leads to a definitive policy answer. The second aspect includes science-based decisions that are not only hard to achieve but are a contradiction in terms. Therefore, the most intractable aspect of incomplete knowledge is considered as ignorance.

It is difficult to predict likelihoods and possibilities. No one can reliably foresee the unpredictable, but can only learn from past mistakes. Dominant paradigms are not always accurate. Knowledge constantly evolves, thriving on scepticism and diversity.

Such scenarios offer the possibility of concrete policy decisions with efficiency. They relate to a decision with available scientific methods that are much clearer and transparent than the political economy sides. Thus instead of seeking definitive generic assessments about risks of particular choices, it is wiser to consider the assumptions behind the scenarios. A constant humility of science-based decisions is always refined by value judgement and experience.

It is important to know the back-cast in history before any forecast. Scenarios such as the seismic, natural, or man-made disasters in record-breaking magnitude, help planners to describe journeys into the future, the road that is less well-travelled and probably not a comfort zone. Scenarios can help technocrats pick some black swan events[4] with more intelligence to strategise and formulate options.

Macroeconomic models for forecasting GDP and other economic parameters are augmented by scenarios from high, medium, and low modalities to harness out-of-box thinking. The Department of Economic Development's econometric model has been projecting official GDP forecasts since 2010. It has baseline, low and high scenarios for policy simulations relating to changes in wages, oil prices, and fiscal policy affecting employment, GDP, and inflation.

Future studies with risk assessment are techniques to look farther beyond economics. Beyond Vision 2030, technology frontiers, emerging sectors, socio-cultural megatrends related to workplace, gender and ageing issues, ethnicity and plurality pose uncertainties and risks. Geopolitics, geoeconomics, the good, bad and ugly side of globalisation continue to change the global competition and marketplace. All these scenarios made Abu Dhabi to join the Look East versus Look West debate, but it needs to optimise a fusion.

---

[4]A black swan event is seemingly a surprise, but has a major impact. After the fact when the event is rationalised by hindsight, a theory emerges as outliers collectively playing a larger role in more regular events (Taleb, 2010, p. xxi). Other future studies include Glenn *et al.*, 1999 and Michel-Kerjan, 2010.

Ironically, the East–West divide in reverse has the developing, emerging world with the financial resources, but technology leadership continues to reside in the West. Unemployment that resulted from the global financial crisis must be addressed immediately and efforts should be undertaken to increase the rate of employment. All countries — Western to India or China — will need to create employment opportunities. But such growth in employment opportunities combined with lower productivity and additional labour inputs may actually increase the inflation rate. This suggests that Abu Dhabi has to be mindful and ready for policy trade-offs.

Vision 2030 as a bold optimistic approach cannot be faulted in being more based on an oasis scenario rather than a desert storm scenario. Charles Handy's (1995) narration of a frog in slowly-boiling water is not forgotten. A prevention-better-than cure approach needs Vision 2030 to be alert, not be complacent that it has a plan in Vision 2030.

One of the important lessons from the Arab Spring is that in a rush to achieve balanced regional development, Abu Dhabi should not forget its Emiratis or leave them behind.

Despite worse scenarios, Abu Dhabi is well-endowed to mitigate its lack of crisis management. It resorted to price and rental caps to tame the inflation in 2007–2008. In 2009, it put up two tranches of $10 billion each as bail-out for Dubai after Dubai World deferred its payment on loans due. Another scenario in 2010 was the UAE's withdrawal from the GCC monetary union due as much to politics as it can afford to forego the benefits of a single currency (Low *et al.*, 2010).

5.5. Abu Dhabi's Economic Development Model

Between aspirations and reality checks, Abu Dhabi Inc manages a small, open economy, with resources mobilised by its visionary leadership — a rarity. Opting for a pace that is comfortable with its more "homeland" culture and legacy, its reliance on migrant labour must morph into a global talent policy commensurate with its population policy. The socialisation process of a global citizenry, not assimilation or integration except for GCC citizens, is a switch from humanitarianism to economism.

Abu Dhabi Inc with its unique DNA and branding is different from other East Asian government-led development models. If Asia has perspiration without inspiration, then Abu Dhabi has plenty of vision, but needs to work hard toward its goals. Being a well-resourced country, the surplus resources can be directly exported as capital in the form of outward direct foreign investment, foreign acquisition, and asset investment to diversify strategically using capable talents. Less direct forms of support include overseas development assistance and remittances as relation-based goodwill.

Privatisation efforts, since the 1980s, by the Abu Dhabi Water and Electricity Authority and General Holding Company, as wealth distribution and capital injection via initial public offers have beefed up its listing in the stock exchange and instilled a shareholder culture. Abu Dhabi Inc is progressively reinvented in public–private partnerships and joint ventures to facilitate rather than merely own, control, and regulate its business.

The government's deployment of capital reflects its keenness for technology transfer from multinational corporations to strengthen the backbone of local family business and small and medium-sized enterprises. The General Holding Company has become a business promoter and developer to practise rolling privatisation by growing clusters, filling gaps and joining the dots together, as the Mudadala Development Company does.

The distinctive role of government-knows-best in the Abu Dhabi brand is in tandem with nurturing private-sector-knows-more as a growth engine in Vision 2030. The private sector is valued for its ears and eyes on the ground to help bureaucrats to gain deeper insight into the industry and the kind of business they do.

Emirati bureaucrats too are allowed to own and operate business. This leads to conflict of interest as the regulator is also the owner. Bureaucrats gain more economic and technical knowledge as part of overall leadership training. Any intervention therefore is pro-entrepreneur and pro-enterprise business.

Regardless of which country model or experience suits, Abu Dhabi's economic development model has to achieve a two-pronged industrial strategy which shows that high value-added, energy-intensive, capital-intensive exports need productivity to weed out low value-added, labour-intensive, and low-skilled activities. Thus the weakest link in human resources development needs mitigation by a people-process-product formulation.

With infrastructure and institutions in place, the industry needs capable and efficient human resources development strategy. Attitude-skills-knowledge (ASK) implies a change in the mindset. The high voluntary unemployment of Emiratis is a symptom, but morphing into a root cause of the 80% migrant reliance and lack of an industrial culture as private sector discipline. To be successfully branded, Abu Dhabi's economic competitiveness and social competitiveness needs productivity-based quality emiratisation.

For publicity, branding, and national identity, the Office of the Brand of Abu Dhabi (http://brand.abudhabi.ae) was formed in 2007. A brand, icon, and initiatives support Vision 2030 while embracing culture and the past as heritage. Oral history such as the recording words of Zayed acts as a glue that forges multi-faceted development which is immortalised in the legacy of Zayed Museum. Even the local knowledge can be mined to build and strengthen a national identity as a new business model emerges.

The Abu Dhabi Tourist Authority was the first to embrace the brand/icon as a framework for gaining reputation and delivering branding solutions for its events and products. The Office of the Brand of Abu Dhabi has commissioned the Sougha Initiative launched by the Khalifa Fund in 2011 to produce branded handmade items. This strategy of reaching out to citizens, protects and enhances the Emirati identity. It draws out support of both the public and private sectors ranging from investment and business culture to social community values.

Enabling Emiratis with special needs means that more job opportunities are created for an inclusive and harmonious society. This human touch, including better industrial relations gradually built for migrant workers is in and of itself *sui generis* for Abu Dhabi's economic development model. A human face is what Zayed Vision has branded, not to be lost among the hard mass of economics and statistics.

Certainly, many hard truths, some self-inflicted paradoxes and reality checks are recognised since Vision 2030 is faced with hard and tough implementation. Decreeing new institutions is not the same nor as simple as building up capacity and capability. It is long-term and hard, mired by a lack of understanding of the lean management concept. Making and amending federal laws with emirate by-laws for execution is in and of itself, another process; worse is in practice, they seldom are as aligned in theory.

Internal factors such as local knowledge of Emiratis comprising drivers and executors, with the political will and commitment to remain on courses are all in the people-process-product equation. Some checks-and-balances of possible over reliance on foreign workers includes consultants who import generic models in wholesale without much adaptation to local conditions and socio-cultural milieu. It takes both knowledge and political courage to choose wisely and avert following foolish projects.

With more risk and uncertainty regionally and globally, more of the same is not enough. The economic template for restructuring and diversification seeks to transform from oil to non-oil economy. The best example for this is Dubai that offers the nearest and dearest case of non-oil and knowledge-based economy. Each case wants a distinct brand to match its reputation, credibility, and image.

Singapore and Hong Kong are pioneering and open, but resource-deficit city-states, and moving up the industrialisation ladder. They reengineer and reinvent as their hinterlands force the pace to the next version. Managing each stage is a challenge-and-response DNA to identify potential opportunities constructively versus East Asian geoeconomics and geopolitics.

Abu Dhabi realises continuous change, often cannot be controlled and paced as assumed when finalising the Vision 2030 document. Everything from internal challenges to external events, including changing scenarios is calibrated except some peculiar contradictions, anomalies or paradoxes. Some of the scenarios are self-inflicted that can only be resolved by the Emiratis themselves like the voluntary unemployment. Tribal capitalism is both the glue and obstacle for national teamwork and that is why the whole-of-government is wholeheartedly ready to execute Vision 2030.

If Abu Dhabi entities can for the first time come together to con-
ceptualise the Vision 2030, then sitting down together again to roll it
out may be both easier and harder. The easy part relates to aligning
the thought process with the actual institutional restructuring.' . . . Yet,
more agencies sprouted only stretches a thin critical mass of Emiratis.

The Secretariat-General tries to relate each entity's plan to contribution to the Vision 2030 as a contingent on the performance of
others. Thus making each agency whether a host or champion in a
cluster means that the Department of Economic Development in key
economic initiatives delivers its mandate only if other stakeholders
contribute and co-operate to work as a national team. This thereby
puts the spirited tribal competition into motion in a constructive
positive-sum game.

This is the difficult side as tribal rivalry is also squeezed by non-
Emiratis all around. It need not unglue national *esprit de corps* of
teamwork with sufficient leaders and change agents to manage the
entropy of spontaneous change, random theory, and chaos theory.
Credit and recognition as implicit mean individuals take pride in
results and internalised self-worth. Mindset of people is more important than manufacturing a product or process in Vision 2030.

The process of one team for further reinvention phases needs
another element. The civil service needs a proper archive for documents,
files, or studies in a central registry in both hard and soft versions.
Institutional memory goes with frequent staff exists and the wheel is
reinvented with fresh recruits. It is literally a cold start despite much
work done by transitory foreign consultants who are happy with more
contracts. This is where knowledge management[5] enters, more than
archiving to mine the accumulated information.

As Abu Dhabi grasps administrative and management best practices,
it could make its branding image stronger and be exemplary to others in
the GCC and MENA countries. In time, Arabic software programmes,
adaptations of Western management systems, appropriately acclimatised

---

[5]Knowledge management is defined as designing and installing techniques and processes to create, protect and use known knowledge as a resource to embody it in
other initiatives and programmes as value-added.

to local needs and work culture can to be multiplied and commercialised as branded Vision 2030 business solutions and products.

A case in point is dealing with population, foreign labour and accompanying emiratisation with an array of policies, laws, and regulations. Sensitivity to local culture, values and heritage, local solutions and best practices as crafted and successfully executed can make Abu Dhabi a part of knowledge-based economy offerings.

Finally, a most unlikely remote, but surprising model is new India[6] which is a riddle at the heart of its rapid growth.[7] Abu Dhabi can learn a few realities. India as a democracy, not India Inc as a private sector does thrive. It has widespread corruption and an inefficient government, especially in infrastructure. Despite of all this, it has shown growth in the economy and some poverty-alleviation because of the profit-motivated private sector. India's answer is that its growth is occurring in spite of, not because of, the government via the private sector.

Whereas Abu Dhabi Inc and China Inc built world-class infrastructure with macroeconomic efficiency, India's micro-efficiency compensates for its macro-inefficiency. In the past decade, it managed to emerge as a new global engine of growth, from call centres or information communication technology graduating into globally competitive Infosys or the Tata Group in industries. In reality, small towns manage in a complete mess to grow as a microcosm of both Indian dynamism and dysfunction.

India's private sector is an engine of growth by default and necessity, not by planning *per se*. Its hardy and sustainable version of economic growth is often a product of private sector which is continuously improvising to overcome the inadequacies of the government. It is the necessity which is the mother of invention. Thus income growth

---

[6] Bangalore is a pioneer city, but others like Gurgaon is among the latest in new India growing beyond the traditional 3% Hindu rate in the 1970s and 1980s to over 9% to match and overtake ageing China at some point, given India's younger, growing 1.2 billion population; *International Herald Tribune*, June 8, 2011.

[7] Equally challenged, Bangladesh has its Grameen Bank to revolutionise microfinance, especially to empower women entrepreneurs as the transmission of progress in both family and rural development.

lifts many out of poverty, economic development follows without hewing to any plan. Equity remains a socio-political issue.

A 2009 seminal article by Jeff Immelt, Head of General Electric, started a frugal innovation,[8] but Indian frugality took it to over the top with pent-up demand that witnessed Tata Motors' $2,200 Nano car, Godrej & Boyce Manufacturing's $70 fridge run on batteries or Narayana Hrudayalaya Hospital offering free heart surgeries in Bangalore.

The tipping point in frugal invention or innovation[9] is a markedly lack of state determination mitigated by a true private sector. It is not just redesigning products, but rethinking the entire production process and business model as total outreach.

A possible virtue out of necessity is for Abu Dhabi tapping Indians as over 40% of its migrant labour. In truth, the Indian DNA for survival and prosperity may balance or, better yet, team up with what Emiratis have taken for granted as their birthright. There are many success cases in retail; why not in creative frugal innovations as well for Vision 2030 to be inclusive of all in Abu Dhabi?

5.6. Conclusions and Policy Implications

Despite the unforeseen global financial crisis and Arab Spring, Vision 2030 is *en route* with some sobering adjustments which are also due to the reality in implementation. Micro-inefficiency notably needs productivity to catch-up for sustainability. Muddling through still contributes positively to the fragile, fragmented, and bifurcated global recovery.

This book is open-ended. Vision 2030 and Abu Dhabi's economic development are still evolving. Some assessment can be surmised, enabling the readers from various nationalities and walks of life

---

[8]Many articles in *The Economist* spot trends in frugal innovations and related open source crowd-sourcing; August 29, 2008, April 8, 2010, August 26, 2010, November 4, 2010, January 27, 2011, and March 17, 2011.

[9]Frugal or constraint-based innovation is more than simply cutting costs to the bone with tough, easy to use multiple-use products. Frugality is not second-rate. The latest technology is a sparing use of raw materials without adverse environmental impact. It is not rocket-science to be frugal with crowd-sourcing. Like the Wikipedia model, ideas multiply and innovations blossom.

to assess the challenge and response. A lot of effort needed is clear in every step, irrespective of the period or target.

By 2030, Abu Dhabi would be mature, industrialised by its branded model whether or not to put the world *en garde*. Small in size, but big in energy, it is *sans* BRIC rhetoric, whether or not it joins the OECD class.

In conclusion, four policy implications are distilled. A caution is Abu Dhabi must always learn the right lesson irrespective of the model, role model or experiences elsewhere. Strategic planning along with scenario planning and future studies plus risk assessment is acceptable beside expecting the unexpected with allowances for ser-endipity. The latter is the chance factor in Porter's five-forces. Thus bracing for storms needs a solid foundation.

One policy implication is a national strategic policy think-tank for multifaceted roles. UAE universities and academic research institutions are not only suppliers of skilled manpower and analysis, but is also the heart of knowledge industries for innovation. The Emirates Centre for Strategic Studies and Research is federally funded with a diverse menu from security to broader social sciences. Thus, more of Abu Dhabi-based technical, science and technology tertiary bodies are discerned.

The ideal is an independent policy research institute, without any conflict of interests. In reality, a state-financed national think-tank is a receptacle for local knowledge and oral history from pioneers in all walks of life. It includes planners, senior bureaucrats and others who are involved in all stages of Vision 2030. An institutionalised archive is in lieu of other entities' lack of a central registry of files, documents, and consultancy reports. The raw research materials for analysis beyond Vision 2030 are preserved, archived for knowledge management.

Much of the literature now is by foreign scholars who could both tap and train Emirati postgraduate students from their academic the-ses to collaborative research after they graduate. This collaboration of foreign brain-ware and local knowledge is similar to the collaboration and cooperation of science and technology with industries. The aca-demia acts as an intellectual partner with industries in a knowledge-based economy for innovation.

The concept is like joint-government training centres for skills upgrading where many multinational research facilities and think-tanks are already producing knowledge to be tapped. Knowledge transfer is more effective than offering pure research grants to foreign academia and intellectual professionals working from their home bases without much interaction with local experts. Online information and statistics or short fly-in-and-out visits are superficial without the alchemy of human bonding.

State-of-the-art research in pure science and technology may be generic, universal, and amenable to distant research partnerships. The methodology in arts, social sciences, and humanities need surveys and *in-situ* observations, not laboratories replicating control sets of experiments. Fieldwork is hard work in any subject. More human face-to-face information gathering is an art more than a science.

Happenings in Abu Dhabi and MENA are attracting global interests. A policy think-tank as an association of universities and institutes is the ultimate form of academic crowd-sourcing, which is facilitated and expedited by information communication technology. Foreign campuses in Abu Dhabi have seeded networks to be bonded with local counterparts. More empirical evidence is always needed for comparative analysis, benchmarking, reviewing, or recalibrating the Vision 2030.

A policy think-tank examines path dependency, scenario planning, and futures study with a strong dose of reality as a strategic pragmatism. Typically, path dependency in policy-making defines a set of systematic and dynamic processes whereby small events have long lasting consequences (Antonelli, 2000). Economic action can modify, but only to a limited extent. Chance events or historical accidents have long-run cumulative consequences (Porteous, 1999).

By an interaction of a variety of agents, path dependency is generated analytically by overlapping irreversibility, indivisibility, and structural change. Change agents choose a successful path which is given to different competing regimes. But path dependency implies some lock-in tendency as technological change tends to be local or due in the past quantitatively and/or qualitatively (David, 1975, 1997).

Since learning occurs primarily around existing techniques, so more advanced society learns to stay at the cutting edge of progress (Mokyr, 1990, p. 163).

Vision 2030 and other GCC plans all diversifying into non-oil knowledge-based economies, are prone to group-thinking by same sets of consultants which is conservatively safe. Even decision-makers sharing some tribal roots, mental paradigms, and orientations tend to apply the same to ideas. Bureaucrats go for safer, proven formulaic strategies and policies. But the first successful experiment becomes the pace-setter.

More specifically, a national policy think-tank can be tasked to seek alternative paradigms or courses of action as differentiated products. Policy-makers have different priorities as domestic politics always prevail over regional or global, but not in a vacuum. This suggests that nothing is neat and tidy in a creative innovation for shifting paradigms or worldviews without a strong efficient state.

Visionary leadership is considered as an instinctive entrepreneurial quality, akin to business gut. Cognitive dissonance means knowing which alternative approaches are not right to be discarded from the outset. Paralysis by analysis, stuck in theoretical research or timidity needs directed policy research. Further study as the age-old code for stasis becomes procrastination, mired by new events a constant change.

A national policy think-tank is pragmatic, practical, and realistic to balance scholarly rigour, but not hide behind jargons and technicalities. Thinking-out-of-the-box is creative, innovative, and opportunistic as Mubadala Development Company was in semiconductors. Proactive and not reactive policy-making needs in-depth research, more than the consultants who outsource that to the academic thinkers and theorists.

A basic amount of confidence and certainty is invested, but not cast in stone in Vision 2030. In order to add value, the proposed think-tank's completed papers or books as peer-reviewed and published, must contribute to the literature. Some are *de facto* living testimony of Vision 2030 as measured, metered, and assessed. Beyond national endogenous factors as population or food security, exogenous scenarios are by sheer propinquity or global interdependence.

A second policy implication is a related concept of an economic string of pearls utilising the think-tank's output. It borrows from China's string of pearls which is both strategic in national security and economic defence.[10] Abu Dhabi Inc is distinctly based on Vision 2030 which is branded with oil wealth and a proactive, aggressive cluster of sovereign wealth funds. The Mubadala Development Company may be a start toward this. It is Vision 2030-plus when extended abroad.

Simply illustrated, direct foreign investment in semiconductor via acquisitions and mergers in Globalfoundries, spans four continents in Europe (Dresden), North America (Saratoga, New York state), Asia (Singapore) and another to be built in Abu Dhabi (MENA). It has locked-in its semiconductor model as geographically more diverse and stable than Taiwan's model comprising two of the world's largest plants. Because of an earthquake in 2006 in Taiwan, it proved to be its Achilles' heel and disrupted the global chip industry.

The theory of a string of pearls for Vision 2030-plus is a virtuous circle of regional dynamics for enterprise diversity, entrepreneurship, technological diversion, and inter-firm networks to ensure competitive and open systems (Best, 2000, p. 462; Borrus *et al.*, 2000). Called variously cross production networks or regional industrial clusters, they allow various niches for specialisation from low to higher value-added goods and intangible services across the whole spectrum.

They are directed by market forces, maximising profit, productivity, efficiency, and competition. A co-location of producers as a partnership of state-owned enterprises and multinational corporations ties in smaller local suppliers with supply chain benefits of technology

---

[10]China's new capabilities extend its reach to the Indian Ocean in a string of pearls from deepwater ports in Pakistan and Bangladesh to roads in Nepal, oil and gas pipelines in Myanmar as supply and commercial routes, like the traditional silk road. Amid South Asian politics, China sells sophisticated weaponry, cheap credit for oil-storage facilities, airports, coal-fired power plants or state-of-the-art performance-arts centres. It is the biggest aid donor for states stigmatised by the West for poor human rights. China's string of pearls is both an economic proposition and for international relations; *The Economist*, August 19, 2010.

transfer. Economies of scale and scope and proximity to markets for all other investors and interests abroad bring home value-added products, without hollowing-out.[11]

Singapore's regionalisation or second-wing policy has tried to replicate its Jurong industrial parks in Batam (Indonesia) Suzhou (China), Bangalore, or Vietnam. A similar string of pearls could work for Abu Dhabis Vision 2030-plus to mitigate its challenges in Vision 2030. The think-tank has to weigh the geoeconomics and geopolitics carefully in many areas.

One is a possible solution to its chronic deficit of skilled labour and human resources development considered as its greatest disadvantage. But a carefully selected string of pearls based on competitiveness and efficiency as a second wing taps both resource supply and market demand abroad. Further, this helps in bringing work-to-workers (abroad) rather than workers-to-work (Abu Dhabi). It could obviate some pressures of the 80% foreign domination and tap the skilled electronics workers as Globalfoundries in Singapore, Dresden, or Saratoga.

Two, for emiratisation, some Emiratis are given the opportunity to head up ventures abroad. This may stretch the deficit of national talents needed at home, but it cannot be underscored that home comforts become a trade-off with working and living abroad as part of life's learning curve in a globally competitive business model.

Three, with or without production networks as part of GCC industrial integration, Abu Dhabi has to promote competitiveness based on regionness or regionality. Then only the foreign investors and multinational corporations would pick up Abu Dhabi as headquarter given its political socio-cultural stability, emerging stride up its industrial ladder, and economic development. But thinking hard on the incentives to attract specific headquarters raises demand for professional business services and other high-value services.

Four, a positive win–win strategy is in remaking the image of sovereign wealth funds which is not seen in land grabs, farmlands for

---

[11]These include side-effects as deindustrialisation or outsourcing with attendant job and income loss, but a chance to move into more core competitive pursuits up the industrial ladder.

food security, or other strategically sensitive areas as threats. The Abu Dhabi Investment Authority has co-chaired and ultimately pioneered in instituting the rules drawn up for corporate governance in the 2009 IMF's working group for sovereign wealth funds. Its string of pearls should convey geoeconomic benefits, not geopolitical threats.

Five, Abu Dhabi's Vision 2030-plus string of pearls as a model for other strategically-minded sovereign wealth funds in the region may enable GCC cooperation and consolidation. A triple-play of wealth is in the OPEC, Organisation for the Islamic Conference (OIC) and a less visible, but rich source of capital amassed as *zakat*. The first two are self-explanatory in global activities.

Extension of the economic string of pearls further deploys the official development assistance. As one of the five pillars of Islam, *zakat* as an accepted practice may be like Islamic finance as a potential pool of funds for mobilisation for economic development. More than charity, philanthropic *zakat* capital is a generic socially-motivated resource with in-built corporate governance and corporate social responsibility.

The UAE disbursed $1,038.2 million in gross official development assistance in 2009. It exceeded those of the six donors in the Development Assistance Committee in the OECD,[12] making it the third largest donor outside the six after Saudi Arabia and China. Most of the aid by the UAE is to the Middle East, followed by South-Central Asia and North Africa. The Abu Dhabi Fund for Development,[13] in particular, for funded projects in Egypt and built Zayed cities and Khalifa cities in South Asia and Indonesia.

Putting it all together, the Abu Dhabi model for economic development extends Vision 2030-plus extraterritorially as a capital exporter. A consolidated string of pearls extends to Vision 2030-plus both in spatial and reputational value so that its credibility grows without the stigma of resource curse to share its blessing abroad. It is

---

[12]The details were provided in 2010 by the UAE as a first time whole-of-government report, also a first by the UAE as a non-OECD member; http://www.oecd.org.
[13]The Abu Dhabi Fund for Development has loans and grants financing 16 Egyptian development and socio-economic projects; *The National*, May 8 and 12, 2011.

not pure altruism as economic defence is as vital as national defence and security for a mature political economy.

When the fixed exchange rate regime switches to a managed float, Abu Dhabi exporting capital as ladling surplus reserves from balance of payments abroad averts appreciation of its currency as hurting exports. This capital export creates jobs opportunities abroad, soothes labour deficit at home to reset a global talent policy. Therefore, its model amplified by like-minded GCC states in economic development changes the total GCC landscape, not by oil alone.

Externalising capacity in oil and gas, semiconductors, or utilities has already begun by this time. South Asia is logical for proximity in geography, culture, and reflecting the stock of South Asian migrants in residence. For the younger migrant generation, they act as a bridge by reacquainting them with their original homes and mediate with their local knowledge of Abu Dhabi.

The policy think-tank can put more thought into an evolving trend to tie up other loose ends as the GCC railway, airways, and electronic highways by simply following the money; literally from remittances to official development assistance. South Asia is a stepping stone; the rest of Asia and beyond becomes truly look-East (Low *et al.*, 2010).

From rags-to-riches as an eighteenth-century sheikdom, the UAE now has assets of worth $1 million, one in every 10 households.[14] As Dubai sustains itself as the most prominent offshore centre in the region, Vision 2030-plus is a compelling proposition for high net wealth individuals to park their asset management needs with Abu Dhabi. A lot of business beckons. Russia to MENA have emerged as the most important origins of offshore wealth; MENA at $4.5 trillion in 2010 rising to $6.7 trillion by 2015.

One ingredient is very clear. Abu Dhabi needs more than change agents in transferring these ideas into reality across-the-board.

---

[14]This is compared to one every 11 households in Qatar. All are dwarfed only by Saudi Arabia with the highest proportion hyper-rich households in the world defined as over $100 million in assets with the UAE, Qatar, and Kuwait among the top 10 in a study by Boston Consulting Group; *The National*, June 5, 2011.

A virtuous circle in one fell swoop needs game changers with the technical and local knowledge of what and how to change or influence scenarios as suited. Game-changing change agents need wide-ranging, in-depth knowledge beyond off-the-charts iconic plans of the consultants. It has more fiscal space than most, defined as room for fiscal allocation to yield the desired results.

A third policy implication that also has to be enriched by the policy think-tank is scenario planning of exogenous X-factors. In trade liberalisation, the UAE is knowledgeable and experienced since it joined the WTO in 1995, relative to Saudi Arabia in 2005. Vision 2030 as a wish-list takes for granted a favourable neighbourhood and regionality in its national competitiveness for free, open trade. This is obviously not the case.

Whether the GCC has any scenario planning is another matter. It has turned 30-year since 1981. Economic integration[15] remains as a mixed bag of failure and success. Without deepening, possible widening has Jordan and Morocco applying, so it pays to have scenarios of a potentially two-track GCC. What does this portends for Vision 2030?

One immediate implication is on labour and capital movement for GCC citizens if voluntary Emirati unemployment persists. A larger GCC may diversify Arabic-speaking GCC and non-GCC nationals as from Lebanon or Egypt for jobs. Even other non-Arabic groups, especially from South Asia and the Philippines may possibly face more competition if not displaced.

Beyond the GCC (Emirates Centre for Strategic Studies and Research, 2008d), rising China (Kleine-Ahlbrandt *et al.*, 2008, McNally, ed, 2008; Qiang, 2009) demands more oil. Rising India

---

[15]Stepwise in theory, economic integration involves, a preferential trade area moving to a free trade area with zero-tariffs, to a customs union with a common external tariff, then a common market with free movement of capital and labour before a monetary union. The GCC may have been blind-sighted by the EU model going the whole way to a currency union. Now, the lessons of Portugal, Ireland, Italy, Greece, and Spain sovereign default as impinging on the rest. In contrast, the UAE like UK opting out of the eurozone can still enjoy the benefits of economic integration without a common currency.

(Moha *et al.*, 2008, Satyendra, 2008; Mazumdar *et al.*, 2008) and its own need for labour have different implications and scenarios for Abu Dhabi to ruminate.

One important scenario or X-factor is inflation. Its sources and types as cost-push, demand-pull, or imported seem as clear as mud in the way the 2007–2008 inflationary episode was handled. In 2011, the Ministry of Economy in Abu Dhabi, in an initiative toward price control until the end-2011, asked the big supermarket chains to subsidise the costs of some 400 products. This approach only tried to focus on the symptoms and treat them, but it did not eradicate the root cause of inflation. Inflation itself has to be properly understood in the first instance; the same is true of basic economics for all policy-making and decisions.

UAE supermarkets ingeniously use their corporate social responsibility funds to pay as compliance. Retailers maintain profits. Consumers generally benefit but not recipients of corporate philanthropy mostly in education, health care, and economic development.

Such misguided measures, on-going labour market restructuring and laws do add to the business cost. Again, the proposition for productivity growth is more compelling. Inflation is better averted by productivity growth as more value-added by higher skilled labour input justifies non-inflationary high wages.

A multicultural civil society will evolve in parallel as Vision 2030 is attained. This acts as the final implication. In and of itself, political and corporate governance will be affected as a civil society grows with more non-government organisations. Carefully crafted, a civil society, more than a civic society comprising non-profit or not-for-profit non-government organisations are needed to enact as a series of corporate social actions.[16]

There are many paths as more than a trade union or a law professional association which Abu Dhabi curiously eschews, but is more responsive to register nature groups. The civil society movement may

---

[16]Both civil society and civic society comprise non-government organisations, focused respectively on civil and/or human rights or purely charitable activities, though the line blurs again as societies are for people as the common denominator.

be politically sensitive because human rights became the *de facto* focus. Instead, a mature society twinning with post-Vision 2030 needs a civil society as much as a knowledge society[17] twins with a knowledge economy. The proposed think-tank can educate, bring awareness, facilitate communication to help better policy-crafting, the basic toolkit for Vision 2030, Vision 2030-plus, and thereafter.

In the 21st century with information communication technology, the civil society morphs and grows with a knowledge society. This is a society in which the creation, dissemination, and utilisation of information and knowledge has become the most important factor of production. A knowledge society contains knowledge assets (intellectual capital) which are the most powerful producer of wealth, more than land, labour and physical or financial capital.

If so, then it is more than the economics of liberalisation and deregulation of broadcasting or media sectors. Content is the hardest to manage as knowledge is neither value-free nor politically neutral. Social development, social transformation and a knowledge-based society for Abu Dhabi, Vision 2030 and beyond will take another book.

---

[17]This is not a new concept. Hayek (1945) had noted that more than a rational economic order allocates given resources to make the best use of resources in planning economic activities. It is more a problem of the utilisation of knowledge which is not given to anyone in its totality.

BIBLIOGRAPHY

Al Abed, I and P Hellyer (eds.) (2001). *UAE in a New Perspective*. UK: Trident Press Ltd.

Abdelal, R. and I Tarsis (2007). *Mubadala: Forging Development in Abu Dhabi*. Harvard Business Review, Prod. #: 708033-PDF-ENG.

Abu Dhabi Department of Economic Development, Studies Directorate (2011). *Report Economic of the Emirate of Abu Dhabi*. Abu Dhabi: Department of Economic Development.

Abu Dhabi Department of Economic Development (2010). *Time to Shine*. Abu Dhabi: Department of Economic Development. http//www.adeconomy.ae.

Abu Dhabi, Department of Planning (various years since 1971). *Statistical Yearbook of Abu Dhabi*. Abu Dhabi: Department of Planning.

Abu Dhabi, Department of Planning and Development (various years since 2009). *Statistical Yearbook of Abu Dhabi 2006*. Abu Dhabi: Department of Planning and Development.

Abu Dhabi, Department of Planning (1996/97). *Household Expenditure Survey*.

Abu Dhabi, Department of Planning and Economy (2008). *Future of Economic Development in Abu Dhabi Toward a Broadened Partnership Between the Public and Private Sectors*. Abu Dhabi: Department of Planning.

Abu Dhabi National Oil Company and Abu Dhabi Department of Economic Development (2010). *The Oil and Gas Year Abu Dhabi 2010*. UK: Wildcat Publishing. http.www.theoilandgasyear.com.

Abu Dhabi, Department of Transport (2009). *Transport Plan*. http//www.abudhabi.ae.

Abu Dhabi, Urban Planning Council (2007). *Plan Abu Dhabi 2030*. Abu Dhabi: Urban Planning Council. http//www.abudhabi.ae.

Abu Dhabi, Statistics Centre (various years, since 2009). *Statistical Yearbook of Abu Dhabi*, (2010). Abu Dhabi: Statistics Centre.

Abdulla, AR (2009). *Policing the Internet in the Arab World*. Occasional Paper, Abu Dhabi: Emirates Centre for Strategic Studies and Research.

Adams, GF, LR Klein, Y Kunasaka and A Shinozaki (2008). *Accelerating Japan's Economic Growth: Resolving Japan's Growth Controversy*. Routledge Studies in the Growth Economies of Asia, Abingdon, Oxon, UK and simultaneously in USA and Canada.

Antonelli, C (2000). *The Microdynamics of Technological Change*. London: Routledge.

Al Faris, AF (ed.) (2001). The *Economy of Abu Dhabi*. Abu Dhabi: Research and Studies Division Publications, Crown Prince Court.

Al-Fahim, M (1998). *From Rags to Riches, The Story of Abu Dhabi*. London: Center for Arabic Studies.

Al Jaber, SA (2008). *An Analysis of Foreign Direct Investment in the United Arab Emirates*. Occasional Paper, Abu Dhabi: Emirates Centre for Strategic Studies and Research.

Barbera, RJ (2009). *Cost of Capitalism: Understanding Market Mayhem and Stabilising Our Economic Future*. New York: McGraw-Hill.

Balakrishnan, MS, P Jayashree and I Michael (eds.) (2010). *Actions and Insights: Business Cases from the UAE*. Dubai: Academy of International Business, Middle East and North Africa, AIB-MENA and University of Wollongong.

Best, GFA (2001), reprint (2006). *Churchill: A Study in Greatness*. London and New York: Hambledon Continuum an Imprint of International Publishing Group.

Best, MH (2001). *The New Competitive Advantage: The Renewal of American Industry*. Oxford: Oxford University Press.

Birchfield, V (1999). Contesting the hegemony of market ideology: Gramsci's "Good Sense" and Polanyi's "Double Movement". *Review of International Political Economy*, 1466–4526, 6(1), 27–54.

Blominvest Bank, SAL (2009). Islamic Banking in the Mena Region. http://www.blominvestbank.com/Library/Files/Islamic%20Banking.pdf.

Boeke, JH (1953). *Economics and Economic Policy of Dual Societies*. New York: Institute of Pacific Relations.

Borrus, M, D Ernst and S Haggard (eds.) (2000). *International Production Networks in Asia: Rivalry or Riches*. London and New York: Routledge.

Brown, RA (2006). *The Rise of the Corporate Economy in Southeast Asia*. London and New York: Routledge.

Brunnermeier, MK (2009). Deciphering the liquidity and credit crunch 2007–2008. *Journal of Economic Perspectives*, 23, 77–100.

Brunnermeier, MK (2001). *Asset Pricing Under Asymmetric Information: Bubbles, Crashes, Technical and Herding*. Oxford: Oxford University Press.

Chu, Y-P and H Hill (eds.) (2006). *The East Asian High-Tech Drive*. Cheltenham: Edward Elgar.

Critchley, RK (2002). *Rewired, Rehired, or Retired? A Global Guide for the Experienced Worker*. San Francisco: Jossey-Bass/Pfeiffer.

Critchley, RK and J Storey (2006). *Rewire or Rust* (revised). San Francisco: Jossey-Bass/Pfeiffer.

Daniels, PW and JW Harrington (eds.) (2007). *Services and Economic Development in the Asia-Pacific*. Aldershot, UK and Burlington, USA: Ashgate Publishing Ltd.

Dash, M (1999, 2000). *Tulipomania: The Story of the World's Most Coveted Flower and the Extraordinary Passions It Aroused*. UK: Victor Gollancz, New York: Three Rivers Press.

David, PA (1975). *Technical Choice, Innovation and Economic Growth: Essays on American and British Experience in the Nineteenth Century*. Cambridge: Cambridge University Press.

David, PA (1997). Path Dependence and the Quest for Historical Economics: One More Chorus of the Ballad of QWERTY. *University of Oxford Discussion Papers in Economic and Social History*, Number 20. http://www.nuff.ox.ac.uk/economics/history/paper20/david3.pdf.

Davidson, MC (2005). *The United Arab Emirates: A Study in Survival — Middle East in the International System*. London: Lynne Rienner Publishers Inc.

Davidson, MC (2009). *Abu Dhabi: Oil and Beyond*. New York: Columbia University Press and London: C Hurst & Co Publishers Ltd.

Dieter, H (2008). *Bilateral Free Trade Agreements in the Asia-Pacific: Problems and Outcomes*. Translated by Adnan Abbas Ali. Abu Dhabi: Emirates Centre for Strategic Studies and Research.

Doganis, R (2001). *The Airline Business in the 21st Century*. London: Routledge.

Drucker, P (1985). *Innovation and Entrepreneurship: Practice and Principles*. New York: Harper & Row.

El Abed, SB (2007). Arabic Language and Culture Amid the Demands of Globalization. *Occasional Paper*, Abu Dhabi: Emirates Centre for Strategic Studies and Research.

El Mallakh, R (1970). The challenge of affluence: Abu Dhabi. *Middle East Journal*, 24(2), Spring, pp. 135–146. http://www.jstor.org/stable/4324581.

El Mallakh, R (1981). *The Economic Development of the United Arab Emirates*. London: Francis & Taylor.

Emirates Centre for Strategic Studies and Research (ed.) (2011). *First Annual Education Conference Proceedings*. Abu Dhabi: Emirates Centre for Strategic Studies and Research.

Emirates Centre for Strategic Studies and Research (ed.) (2010a). *Energy Security in The Gulf: Challenges And Prospects*. Abu Dhabi: Emirates Centre for Strategic Studies and Research.

Emirates Centre for Strategic Studies and Research (ed.) (2010b). *Human Resources and Development in the Arabian Gulf*. Abu Dhabi: Emirates Centre for Strategic Studies and Research.

Emirates Centre for Strategic Studies and Research (ed.) (2010c). *Education and the Requirements of the GCC Labor Market*. Abu Dhabi: Emirates Centre for Strategic Studies and Research.

Emirates Centre for Strategic Studies and Research (ed.) (2009a). *Nuclear Energy in the Gulf*. Abu Dhabi: Emirates Centre for Strategic Studies and Research.

Emirates Centre for Strategic Studies and Research (ed.) (2009b). *The Arabian Gulf: Between Conservatism and Change*. Abu Dhabi: Emirates Centre for Strategic Studies and Research.

Emirates Centre for Strategic Studies and Research (ed.) (2008a). *Future Arabian Gulf Energy Sources: Hydrocarbon, Nuclear or Renewable?* Abu Dhabi: Emirates Centre for Strategic Studies and Research.

Emirates Centre for Strategic Studies and Research (ed.) (2008b). *China, India and the United States: Competition for Energy Resources*. Abu Dhabi: Emirates Centre for Strategic Studies and Research.

Emirates Centre for Strategic Studies and Research (ed.) (2008c). *Globalisation in the 21st Century: How Interconnected is the World?* Abu Dhabi: Emirates Centre for Strategic Studies and Research.

Emirates Centre for Strategic Studies and Research (ed.) (2008d). *Arabian Gulf Security: Internal and External Challenges*. Abu Dhabi: Emirates Centre for Strategic Studies and Research.

Emirates Centre for Strategic Studies and Research (ed.) (2007a). *Gulf Oil and Gas: Ensuring Economic Security*. Abu Dhabi: Emirates Centre for Strategic Studies and Research.

Emirates Centre for Strategic Studies and Research (ed.) (2007b). *Current Transformations and Their Potential Role in Realising Change in the Arab World*. Abu Dhabi: Emirates Centre for Strategic Studies and Research.

Everett, MR (1995). *Diffusion of Innovations.* 4th edn. New York: Free Press.

Evans, A and J von Braun (2009). *Global Food Crisis.* Abu Dhabi: Emirates Centre for Strategic Studies and Research.

Executive Council, Government of Abu Dhabi, Abu Dhabi (2007). Policy Agenda 2007–2008 The Emirate of Abu Dhabi. http//www.abudhabi. ae.

Fan, QM, KQ Li, DZH Zeng, Y Dong and RZ Peng (eds.) (2009). *Innovation for Development and the Role of Government: A Perspective from the East Asia and Pacific Region.* Washington DC: World Bank.

Fischer, S (2005). Central Bank lessons from the Global crisis. *In IMF Essays from a Time of Crisis: The International Financial System, Stabilization, and Development,* S Fischer (ed.). Cambridge: Massachusetts Institute of Technology Press.

Fousekis, P (1997). Internal and external scale effects in productivity analysis: A dynamic dual approach. *Journal of Agricultural Economics,* 48(1–3), 151–166.

Forstenlechner, I and Kamel, M (2010a). Gaining legitimacy through hiring local workforce at a premium: The case of MNEs in the United Arab Emirates. *Journal of World Business,* Elsevier Inc. doi:10.1016/j.jwb. 2010.10.006. www.elsevier.com/locate/jwb.

Forstenlechner, I, M Kamel and E Rutledge (2010b). Unemployment in the Gulf: Time to update the social contract. *Middle East Policy,* 17(2), Summer.

Forstenlechner, I, M Kamel, M Madi, HM Selim and E Rutledge (2011c), forthcoming. Emiratisation: Determining the factors that influence the recruitment decisions of employers in the UAE. *The International Journal of Human Resource Management,* 22(2).

Gorton, G (2008). *The Panic of 2007.* New York: National Bureau of Economic Research.

Gorton, G (2010). *Slapped by the Invisible Hand: The Panic of 2007.* Oxford: Oxford University Press.

Ghani, E, A Grover and H Kharas (eds.) (2010). *The Service Revolution in South Asia.* Oxford: Oxford University Press.

Ghani, E, A Grover and H Kharas (2011). *Service with a Smile: A New Growth Engine for Poor Countries.* VoxEU. http://www.voxeu.org/index. php?q=node/6459.

Glenn, JC and GJ Theodore (1999). *Global Normative Scenarios.* Originally Published by the American Council for the United Nations University in

Cooperation with The Foundation for the Future. http://www.millen-nium-project.org/millennium/scenarios.html.

Goujon, A and B Barakat (2010). Future demographic challenges in the Arab World. *Occasional Paper*, Abu Dhabi: Emirates Centre for Strategic Studies and Research.

Government of Abu Dhabi (2008). The Abu Dhabi Economic Vision 2030, Developed by General Secretariat, Department of Planning and Economy and Abu Dhabi Council for Economic Development. http//www.abud-habi.ae.

Govindarajan, V and C Trimble (2010). *The Other Side of Innovation: Solving the Execution Challenge.* Dartmouth, UK: Tuck School of Business at Dartmouth College.

Hadi, G (2006). *Building Towers, Cheating Workers: Exploitation of Migrant Construction Workers in the United Arab Emirates*, Vol. 18, Human Rights Watch.

Hammer, M and J Champy *(1995). Reengineering the Corporation.* London: Nicholas Brealey.

Handy, CB (1995). *The Age of Unreason.* 2nd edn. London: Arrow.

Heller, P (2005). Understanding Fiscal Space, *IMF Policy Paper* No PDP/05/04, IMF: Washington DC.

Hayek, F (1945). The use of knowledge in a society. *American Economic Review*, 35(4), September, pp. 519–530.

Hall, H (ed.) (2002). *The Economic Development of Southeast Asia*, Vols. I to IV. Cheltenham: Edward Elgar Publishing.

Hyman, PM (1986). *Stabilizing an Unstable Economy: A Twentieth Century Fund Report.* Yale: Yale University Press.

International Monetary Fund (various years). UAE Country Report and UAE Statistical Appendix. IMF and UAE Ministry of Economy websites.

Istaitieh, AA (2008). A Japan–UAE FTA: Analysis and Benefits. *Occasional Paper*, Abu Dhabi: Emirates Centre for Strategic Studies and Research.

Jurong International Consulting, Low, L *et al.* (2004). *Economic Development Plan Industrial Development* (comprising five books, Book 1 on *Market and Business Study Report*; Book 2 on *Industrial Planning Study*; Book 3 on *Infrastructure and Facilities Study*; Book 4 on *Institutional Set-up*; and Book 5 on *Industrial Estate Operations Handbook*). Singapore: Jurong International Consulting.

Jurong International Consulting, Low, L *et al.* (2004). *Foreign Worker Policy for Abu Dhabi.* Singapore: Jurong International Consulting.

Jurong International Consulting, Low, L *et al.* (2005). Abu Dhabi Industrial Development Consultancy (comprising four books, Book 1 on the *Economic Development Plan*; Book 2 on *Industrial Development Plan*; Book 3 on *Advisory on the Specialised Agencies Set-up*; and Book 4 on *Advisory on the Financial Sustainability of Industrial Estate Operations*). Singapore: Jurong International Consulting.

Kakabadse, MOA, R Abouchakra and AQ Jawad (2011). *Leading Smart Transformation*. Houndsmith, UK: Palgrave Macmillan.

Kashyap, AK, R Berner and CAE Goodhart (2010). The macroprudential toolkit, Chicago booth initiative on Global Markets. *Chicago Booth Research Paper*, No. 11–02.

Khun, T (1962, 1996). *The Structure of Scientific Revolutions*. Chicago: University of Chicago Press, 3rd edn.

Kindleberger, CP (1977). The financial instability hypothesis: Capitalistic processes and the behavior of the economy. In *Financial Crises: Theory, History, and Policy*, CP Kindleberger and JP Laffargue (eds.). New York: Wiley International.

Kindleberger, CP (1978). *Mania, Panics and Crashes: A History of Financial Crisis*. New York: Basic Books.

Kirk, D (2010). The Development of Higher Education in the United Arab Emirates, Emirates Centre for Strategic Studies and Research, Occasional Paper, Abu Dhabi: Emirates Centre for Strategic Studies and Research.

Knight, F (1921). *Risk, Uncertainty, and Profit*. Boston, MA: Hart, Schaffner & Marx; Houghton Mifflin Co.

Kleine-Ahlbrandt, S, JL Thornton and A Small (2008). *Changing China: The Prospects for Democracy in China and a New Diplomacy Towards "Rogue States"*. Abu Dhabi: Emirates Centre for Strategic Studies and Research.

Koh, BS (ed.) (2002). *Heart Work: Stories of How EDB Steered the Singapore Economy from 1961 into the 21st Century*. Singapore: Economic Development Board. (Lead author is Chan Chin Bock, contributors, AK Hua, *et al.*).

Krugman, P, M Fujita and A Venables (1999). *The Spatial Economy — Cities, Regions and International Trade*. Cambridge: Massachusetts Institute of Technology Press.

Kuckiki, A and M Tsuji (eds.) (2010). *From Agglomeration to Innovation: Upgrading Industrial Clusters in Emerging Economies*. Houndsmith, UK: Palgrave Macmillan.

Kuran, T (2010). *The Long Divergence: How Islamic Law Held Back the Middle East*. Princeton: Princeton University Press.

Lewis, WA (1954). *Economic Development with Unlimited Supply of Labour*. The Manchester School of Economic and Social Studies, 22, 139–191.

Lim, MMH and C Lim, (2010). *Nowhere to Hide: The Global Financial Crisis and Challenges for Asia*. Singapore: Institute of Southeast Asian Studies.

Low, L, MH Toh, TW Soon and KY Tan (with special contribution from Helen Hughes) (1993). *Challenge and Response: Thirty Years of the Economic Development Board*. Singapore: Times Academic Press.

Low, L (2000a). *Economics of Information Technology and the Media*. Singapore: World Scientific Press and Singapore University Press.

Low, L (2000b). *Education, Skills Training and National Development: Experience and Lessons from Singapore*. Tokyo: Asian Productivity Organisation.

Low, L and DM Johnston (eds.) (2001). *Singapore Inc: Public Policy Options in The Third Millennium*. Singapore: Asia Pacific Press.

Low, L (2002). The limits of a city-state: Or are there? In *Southeast in the New Millennium*, D da Cunha (ed.), pp. 1–25. Singapore: Institute of Southeast Asian Studies.

Low, L (2004). Policy Lessons in Development: Small, Open Economies of Singapore and Abu Dhabi in the United Arab Emirates. *Institute of Southeast Asian Studies Working Paper*, Economics & Finance Series No. 2 (2004).

Low, L (ed.) (2004). *Developmental States: Relevancy, Redundancy or Reconfiguration?* New York: Nova Science.

Low, L (2005). Entrepreneurship development in Ireland and Singapore. *Journal of The Asia Pacific Economy*, 10(1), February, pp. 116–138.

Low, L (2006). *The Political Economy in a City-State Revisited*. Singapore: Marshall Cavendish International.

Low, L and TC Aw (2004). *Social Insecurity in the New Millennium: The Central Provident Fund in Singapore*. Singapore: Marshall Cavendish International.

Low, L and LC Salazar (2010). *Gulf Cooperation Council: The Rising Power and Lessons for ASEAN*. Singapore: Institute of Southeast Asian Studies, ASEAN Study Centre.

Lupia, A and SP Tasha (2007). *Opinions on the Net: The Role of Websites in Generating Political Interest Among the Youth*. Abu Dhabi: Emirates Centre for Strategic Studies and Research.

McNally, CA (ed.) (2008). *China's Emergent Political Economy: Capitalism in the Dragon's Lair*. Routledge Studies in the Growth Economies of Asia, Abingdon, Oxon, UK and simultaneously in USA and Canada.

Mazumdar, D and S Sarkar (2008). *Globalization, Labour Markets and Inequality in India*, Routledge Studies in the Growth Economies of Asia, Abingdon, Oxon, UK and simultaneously in USA and Canada.

Mann, CC (2008). *Abu Dhabi: Birth of an Oil Shaikhdom*. Beirut: Lebanese Books Inc.

Mashood, N, H Verhoeven and B Chansarkar, undated, Emiratisation, Omanisation and Saudisation-common causes: Common solutions? http://www.wbiconpro.com/Helen-UAE.pdf.

McCrohan, D, MS Erogul, N Vellinga and QX Tong (2009). *Global Entrepreurship Monitor Report on Entrepreneurship in the United Arab Emirates*. Abu Dhabi: Zayed University.

Mercator Fund and International Council on Security and Development (2011). Unemployed Youth in the UAE: Personal Perceptions and Recommendations. http://www.mercatorfund.net/ICOS_Unemployed_Youth_UAE Report.zip.

Michel-Kerjan, E and P Slovic (eds.) (2010). *The Irrational Economist: Making Decisions in a Dangerous World*. Washington: DC: Public Affairs Press.

Middle East Economic Digest (2006). *Special Report on Telecommunications*. 25–31 August.

Middle East Economic Digest (2010). *Special Report on Aluminium*. 7–13 May.

Mohan, R, AB Carter, S Ganguly and G Das (2008). *The Rise of India*. Abu Dhabi: Emirates Centre for Strategic Studies and Research.

Mokyr, J (1990). *The Lever of Riches: Technological Creativity and Economic Progress*. Oxford: Oxford University Press.

Myint, H and AO Krueger (2009). *Economic Development*. Encyclopædia Britannica.

Naisbitt, J (1982). *Megatrends*. New York: Warner Books.

Oshima, HT (1963). The Ranis-Fei model of economic development: Comment. *The American Economic Review*, 53(3), 448–452.

Oxford Business Group (2006). *Emerging Abu Dhabi 2006*, various years thereafter. London: Oxford Business Group.

Palacios, JJ (ed.) (2009). *Multinational Corporations and the Emerging Network Economy in Asia and the Pacific*. Routledge, Abingdon.

Petri, PA and SJ La Croix (2007). *Challenges to the Global Trading System: Adjustment to Globalization in the Asia-Pacific Region*. London and New York: Routledge.

Pirie, I (2008). *The Korean Developmental State*, Routledge Studies in the Growth Economies of Asia, Abingdon, Oxon, UK and simultaneously in USA and Canada.

Polanyi, K (1957). *The Great Transformation: The Political and Economic Origins of Our Time*. Boston: Beacon Press.

Porter, ME (1980). *Competitive Strategy*. New York: Free Press.

Porter, ME (2008). The Five Competitive Forces That Shape Strategy. *Harvard business Review*, January.

Porteous, D (1999). The Development of Financial Centres: Location, Information Externalities and Path Dependence. In *Money and the Space Economy*, R Martin (ed.), pp. 95–137. Chichester: Wiley.

Qiang, CZ-W (2009). *China's Information Revolution: Managing the Economic and Social Transformation*. Abingdon: Routledge.

Ranis, G, F Stewart and A Ramirez (2000). Economic growth and human development, *World Development*, 28(2), 197–219.

Reinhart, C and K Rogoff (2009). *This Time is Different: Eight Centuries of Financial Folly*. Princeton: Princeton University Press.

Rutledge, E (2009). GCC Monetary Union: A Cost–Benefit Analysis. *Occasional Paper*, Abu Dhabi: Emirates Centre for Strategic Studies and Research.

Satyendra, SN (2008). *Globalization and the Indian Economy: Roadmap to Convertible Rupee*. Routledge Studies in the Growth Economies of Asia, Abingdon, Oxon, UK and simultaneously in USA and Canada.

Saw, SH and Low, L (2009). Sovereign Wealth Funds, Singapore: Saw Financial Centre. *Financial Studies Series* No. 7, National University of Singapore.

Schein, EC (1996). *Strategic Pragmatism: The Culture of Singapore's Economics Development Board*. Cambridge: Massachusetts Institute of Technology.

Schumpeter, J and U Backhaus (2003). *The Theory of Economic Development*. JA Schumpeter, pp. 61–116. Available at: http://dx.doi.org/10.1007/0-306-48082-4_3.

Sharpley, R (2002). The challenges of economic diversification through tourism: The case of Abu Dhabi. *International Journal for Tourism Research*, 4, 221–235, Wiley Interscience, www.wileyinterscience.com, http//onlinelibrary.wiley, doi: 10.1002, jtr378, 10 Apr.

Shin, J-S and M Lee (2008). *The Korean Economic System: Governments, Big Business and Financial Institutions*. Aldershot: Ashgate Publishing Ltd.

Steil, B and S Dunaway (2009). *The Global Financial Crisis*. Abu Dhabi: Emirates Centre for Strategic Studies and Research.

Suleiman, AI (2007). *The Petroleum Experience of Abu Dhabi*. Abu Dhabi: Emirates Centre for Strategic Studies and Research.

Taleb, NN (2010). *The Black Swan*, 2nd edn. Harlow, UK: Penguin.

Taplin, R (ed.) (2008). *Outsourcing and Human Resource Management, an International Survey*. Routledge Studies in the Growth Economies of Asia, Abingdon, Oxon, UK and simultaneously in USA and Canada.

Taylor, I (2007). *China's Oil Diplomacy in Africa*. Abu Dhabi: Emirates Centre for Strategic Studies and Research.

Toledo, H (2009). Arab Sovereign Wealth Funds and Their Political Implications. *Occasional Paper*, Abu Dhabi: Emirates Centre for Strategic Studies and Research.

Turner, BS (ed.) (2010). *The Routledge International Handbook of Globalization Studies*. New York and Abingdon: Routledge.

UAE Central Bank (various years). *Annual Reports*. Abu Dhabi: UAE Central Bank.

UAE Ministry of Information and Culture (various years over a decade). *UAE Yearbook*. UK: Trident Press and UAE: National Media Council.

UAE Ministry of Economy (2006). *Foreign Direct Investment 2005–2006*. UAE: Ministry of Economy.

UAE Ministry of Foreign Trade (2010). *Trade Policy Review United Arab Emirates 2010*. UAE: Ministry of Foreign Trade.

United Nations (1999). *Abu Dhabi Supply and Use Tables for the Year 1995*. Technical Report No. 18, UNDP/UNDESA Project UAE/96/005 Strategic Development Program, Abu Dhabi (2000–2020), August.

United Nations Development Programme (2010). *Human Development Report 2010, 20th Anniversary Edition*, various years thereafter. New York: UNDP.

Urata, S, SY Chia and F Kimura (eds.) (2006). *Multinationals and Economic Growth in East Asia: Foreign Direct Investment, Corporate Strategies and National Economic Development*. Abingdon: Routledge.

Van Esveld, B (2009). *The Island of Happiness: Exploitation of Migrant Workers on Saadiyat Island, Abu Dhabi*. Human Rights Watch.

Van Foreest, F (2011). Does Natural Gas Need a Decarbonisation Strategy? The Cases of the Netherlands and the UK, *Oxford Institute for Energy Studies Working Paper*, http://www.oxfordenergy.org/2011/05/does-natural-gas-need-a-decarbonisation-strategy-the-cases-of-the-netherlands-and-the-uk/.

Wiseman, AW (2011). Impact of Science Education on the GCC Labor Market. *Occasional Paper*, Abu Dhabi: Emirates Centre for Strategic Studies and Research.

World Bank (various years). *Doing Business Report*. Washington DC: World Bank.

World Economic Forum (various years). *Global Competitiveness Report.* Lausanne, Switzerland: World Economic Forum.

Xu, Y-C and G Bahgat (eds.) (2010). *The Political Economy of Sovereign Wealth Funds.* Houndmills, UK: Palgrave Macmillan.

Yuan, L-T and L Low (1990). *Local Entrepreneurship in Singapore: Private and State.* Singapore: Times Academic Press for Institute of Policy Studies, translated into Japanese by Ikuo Iwasaki, Singapore: Institute of Policy Studies.

Yusuf, S, K Nabeshima and S Yamashita (eds.) (2008). *Growing Industrial Clusters in Asia: Serendipity and Science.* Washington DC: World Bank.

Websites

Abu Dhabi, Airport Business Park, http//www.adfaz.ae.

Abu Dhabi Council for *Economic Development,* http//www.adced.ae.

Abu Dhabi Chamber of Commerce and Industry, http//www.abudhabichamber.ae.

Abu Dhabi Department of Economic Development, http//www.adeconomy.ae.

Abu Dhabi, Department of Transport, http//www.abudhabi.ae.

Abu Dhabi Fund for *Development,* http//www.adfd.ae.

Abu Dhabi Government, official websites, http//www.abudhabi.ae.

Abu Dhabi, Higher Corporation for Specialised Economic Zones, http//www.zonescorp.com.

Abu Dhabi Khalifa Fund for Enterprise Development, http//www.khalifafund.gov.ae.

Abu Dhabi National Media Council, http://www.uaeinteract.com.

Abu Dhabi National Oil Company, http//www.adnoc.ae.

Abu Dhabi, Statistics Centre, http//www.scad.ae.

Abu Dhabi Basic Industries Corporation, http//www.adbic.ae.

Abu Dhabi, Urban Planning Council, http//www.abudhabi.ae.

Emirates Centre for Strategic Studies and Research, http://www.ecssr.ae.

Emirates Aluminium, http//www.emal.ae.

Gulf News, http//www.gulfnews.com.

International Monetary Fund, http//www.imf.org.

Khaleej Times, http//www.khaleejtimes.com.

Khalifa Fund for Enterprise Development, http://www.khalifafund.gov.ae.

Khalifa Port and Industrial Zone, http//www.kizad.ae.

Mubadala Development Company, http//www.mubadala.ae.
The Economist, http//www.economist.com.
The National, http//www.thenational.com.
Tourism *Development* and Investment Company, http//www.tdic.ae.
UAE government official websites, http//www.uae.ae.
UAE free zones, http//www.uaefreezones.ae.
Western Region *Development* Council, http//www.wrdc.ae.
World Bank, http//www.worldbank.org.
World Trade Organisation, http//www.wto.org.

INDEX

Aabar Investments   29
Abu Dhabi Airport Free Zone   45
Abu Dhabi Authority for Culture
  and Heritage   35
Abu Dhabi Basic Industries
  Corporation   37
Abu Dhabi Chamber of Commerce
  and Industry   12
Abu Dhabi Council for Economic
  Development   12
Abu Dhabi Education Council   31
Abu Dhabi Emiratisation
  (Tawteen) Council   109
Abu Dhabi Investment
  Authority   48
Abu Dhabi Municipality   85
Abu Dhabi National Energy
  Company   26
Abu Dhabi National Exhibition
  Company   82
Abu Dhabi National Oil
  Company   25
Abu Dhabi Ports Company   43
Abu Dhabi Stock Market   37
Abu Dhabi Tourism Authority   37
Abu Dhabi Trade House   37

Abu Dhabi Water and Electricity
  Authority   31
Advanced Technology Investment
  Company   53
agglomeration   37
Al Ain   35
Al Gharbia   35
Arab Spring   2
Arkan Building Materials
  Company   12

Bank of International
  Settlements   71
Basel   71
beach-head   89
black swan   146
book-building   81
Borouge   27
BRICS   4
buddy   57
business model   115

change agent   17
Chemaweyaat   45
China   4
cluster   37

comparative advantage   134
competition law   127
continuous education and
   training   95
credit bureau   70
credit rating bureau   70

Department of Economic
   Development   12
Department of Finance   21
Department of Transport   21
direct foreign investment   18
DNA   141
Dolphin   29
double bottomline   51
du   45
dual   23

economic development   2
Economic Development
   Strategic Plan   40
economic growth   2
economies of scale   17
economies of scope   17
Emirates Aluminium (Emal)   44
Emirates Nuclear Energy
   Corporation   34
Emirates Standardisation
   and Metrology Authority   123
Emiratis   14
emiratisation   54
energy capital   3
Entrepôt   15
entrepreneurs   35
entrepreneurship   54
Environmental Agency
   Abu Dhabi   31
etisalat   45

EU   10
Executive Affairs Authority   12
Executive Council   12
export credit   68

fatwas   87
Federal   5
Federal Authority for Nuclear
   Regulation   34
Federal Human Resources
   Authority and Emirates
   Council for Emiratisation
   109
Financial innovations   118
flying geese   64
foreign economic policy   126
foreign worker policy   105
Full employment   102
Future studies   146

GATS   64
GCC   11
General Holding Company   13
General Secretariat   21
Globalfoundries   53
global talent policy   106
government bonds   80
Government Industrial
   Corporation   13
Government-knows-best   13
group-think   156

hawala   107
Higher Colleges of
   Technology   56
holistic, integrated and
   systemic   61
human resources development   3

IMF   19
immigration policy   97
India   4
Industrial City of Abu Dhabi   46
industrial policy   18
inflation   121
Infrastructural Fund   46
initial public offers   13
input–output   8
intellectual property rights   54
International Petroleum
   Investment Company   26
Ireland   18
IRENA   32
Islamic banking   74

Japan   64

Khalifa Fund   11
Khalifa Port Industrial Zones
   43
Kizad   43
knowledge-based   3
knowledge management   151

labour force participation   102

Manpower-Cum-Education
   Planning   58
Masdar   25
Media Zone Authority   45
MENA   10
military-defence complex   55
mindset   98
minimum wages   104
mismatch   98
missing markets   7
model   3

monetising   13
moral hazard   110
Mubadala Development
   Company   29
multinationals corporations   18

national identity   15
New Zealand   18
Norway   18

OECD   4
Office of the Brand of Abu
   Dhabi   149
OIC   159
OPEC   26
outsource   58

paradox   15
paralysis by analysis   156
path dependency   155
peg   68
Petrodollar   17
Petroleum Institute   55
political economy   3
population policy   96
Porter's five-forces   13
Private equity   78
private-sector-knows-more   13
privatisation   8
productivity   10
public–private partnerships   13

reengineer   13
regionness   64
remittances   74
research and development   13
resource curse   2
restructuring   11

Saadiyat Island   66
scenario   8
Science, Technology and
   Innovation Policy   54
S-curve   7
securitisation   72
serendipity   154
Shariah   73
shorting   72
Singapore   27
small and medium-sized
   enterprises   11
social profit   51
sole agency law   120
sovereign wealth funds   16
Statistics Centre Abu Dhabi   21
Strait of Homuz   27
string of pearls   74
succession   115
sukuk   73
Supreme Petroleum Council   25
sustainable   34

Tacaamol   45
takaful   73
Tanmia   109
Taqa   26
Taweelah   47
technoglobalism   55
Technology Development
   Committee   54
technonationalism   55
Telecommunications Regulatory
   Authority   45

think-tank   154
Tourism Development and
   Investment Company   82
trade-off   147
trade policy   125
tribal   5
Trucial States   1
twofour54   43

UAE Academy   109
UAE Offsets Group   29
UAE University   99
UAE Vision 2021   6
UNDP   6
Urban Planning Council   21
usufruct   42

value chain   16
vicious circle   17
virtual states   66
virtuous circle   17
Vision 2030   2
voluntary unemployment   102

wasta   109
weakest link   3
whole-of-government   40
work culture   103
worker residential cities   37
World Bank   55

Zayed University   99
Zayed Vision   1
Zonescorp   36